Seriously Messy

The Bible Reading Fellowship
15 The Chambers, Vineyard
Abingdon OX14 3FE
brf.org.uk

The Bible Reading Fellowship (BRF) is a Registered Charity (233280)

ISBN 978 0 85746 823 9
First published 2019
10 9 8 7 6 5 4 3 2 1 0
All rights reserved

Acknowledgements
Unless otherwise acknowledged, scripture quotations are from The New Revised Standard
Version of the Bible, Anglicised edition, copyright © 1989, 1995 by the Division of Christian
Education of the National Council of the Churches of Christ in the United States of America.
Used by permission. All rights reserved.

Scripture quotations marked RSV are from The Revised Standard Version of the Bible, copyright
© 1946, 1952, 1971 by the Division of Christian Education of the National Council of the Churches
of Christ in the United States of America. Used by permission. All rights reserved. • Scripture
quotations marked KJV are from the Authorised Version of the Bible (The King James Bible), the
rights in which are vested in the Crown, are reproduced by permission of the Crown's Patentee,
Cambridge University Press. • Scripture quotations marked NIV are from The Holy Bible, New
International Version (Anglicised edition) copyright © 1979, 1984, 2011 by Biblica. Used by
permission of Hodder & Stoughton Publishers, a Hachette UK company. All rights reserved.
'NIV' is a registered trademark of Biblica. UK trademark number 1448790. • Scripture quotations
markred TLB are from The Living Bible copyright © 1971 by Tyndale House Foundation. Used by
permission of Tyndale House Publishers Inc., Carol Stream, Illinois 60188. All rights reserved. •
Scripture quotations marked NIRV are from the Holy Bible, New International Reader's Version®.
Copyright © 1996, 1998 Biblica. All rights reserved throughout the world. Used by permission
of Biblica. • Scripture quotations marked CEV are from the Contemporary English Version. New
Testament © American Bible Society 1991, 1992, 1995. Old Testament © American Bible Society
1995. Anglicisations © British & Foreign Bible Society 1996. Used by permission.

Every effort has been made to trace and contact copyright owners for material used in this
resource. We apologise for any inadvertent omissions or errors, and would ask those concerned
to contact us so that full acknowledgement can be made in the future.

A catalogue record for this book is available from the British Library

Printed and bound by CPI Group (UK) Ltd, Croydon CR0 4YY

Seriously Messy

Making space for families to talk
together about death and life

Joanna Collicutt, Lucy Moore,
Martyn Payne and Victoria Slater

DIOCESE *of* OXFORD
A Christ-like Church for the sake of God's world

Contents

PART III: SESSION MATERIAL

Why we wrote this book

What's this? A book about death! A book for parents and grandparents... and children? You can't be serious!

Well, yes, we are. So, let us attempt to tell you why.

Talking of death and dying is one of those conversation topics most of us prefer to avoid – and for good reason. No one wants to be reminded that our life has to end one day. It's something we assign to the distant future – as far away as possible, in fact, so we can conveniently and hopefully forget that the day will ever arrive.

Even within church circles, Christians are often strangely reluctant to talk about death. This is especially odd when Christianity has as its central symbol the cross, which forcibly reminds us that 'Christ has died' and challenges us to 'take up our cross' – our dying – so that we might live. We can't get around this by simply spiritualising those words and thereby hoping to overlook the reality of the deaths involved, both for Christ and ultimately for us.

An awareness of our inevitable death and our attitudes towards it ought to have a huge influence on how we live our lives now. We can't have life without death, and ignoring or denying questions about death and dying is not only unhelpful but is an unhealthy response to God's gift of life to us all. When St Benedict wrote his monastic rule for his followers in the sixth century, he included the line, 'Keep death always before one's eyes.'[1] This was not because he wanted them or us to be morbid killjoys but because by facing up to the natural boundary to our earthly life, we would be much more likely to use our time well and become daily more dependent on Christ, who holds 'the keys of Death' (Revelation 1:18).

Nevertheless, in western culture in particular, we prefer not to talk of death; ageing and terminal illness are largely off limits. In our increasingly secular society, death is viewed as a defeat and a failure – a cause for despair, not hope. By contrast, the Christian faith does not give physical death the last word. Faith in God offers eternal life that goes beyond our bodily death, so there is hope. To talk about death before the end finally comes, whenever and however that happens, is therefore definitely part of our Christian discipleship, and this book offers the theory and the tools to do just that.

Is this a specialist book, then? Is it just for those facing terminal illness or dealing with bereavement?

NO. While the book may be helpful to people (adults and children) for whom death has come close, it's aimed at everybody. It's about bringing the reality of death in a healthy way into the everyday life of the whole church family – young and old, sick and well, fit and frail – so that we can live more fully now.

Okay, but you also claim that this is a book for families with their children? Is the subject matter really appropriate? Surely if any book needs an 18 certificate, then it is one about death and dying, whether the readers are Christian or not? And what's more, you offer this to us with Messy Church sessions on the theme – activities and celebration ideas on death for all ages together: have the authors lost the plot?

On the contrary, the authors firmly believe that an intergenerational setting, such as Messy Church, is exactly the place to talk about the hard questions of life. It is far too easy at such church 'family' gatherings simply to stay with the cosier and relatively easy stories linked to our faith – ones that don't ask awkward questions or open up the big issues of existence. And are we not surely in danger of being unfaithful to the gospel if we play down or, even worse, cut out all the hard sayings and difficult themes that are present in almost every Bible story? If the good news is simply reduced to statements like 'Pray and all will be well' or 'Don't worry, God will make it right again', we are being dishonest in our ministry and mission. It will mean that our children and their parents will grow up with an incomplete understanding of Christianity – one that has Photoshopped out challenging questions about suffering, pain, death and dying.

It is as if we think that God isn't big enough to cope with our doubts and fears in these areas, or even that faith is no longer relevant when things turn out badly and the people we love aren't healed but die. The truth is that those are exactly the moments when we need our faith to carry us through, yet that can only happen if we have been honest enough to talk about these things beforehand. Death and dying need to become part of our shared conversations whenever we meet to celebrate God's presence and when together we determine to listen to what God is saying to us. As we do this in an intergenerational setting, such as in Messy Church or similar shapes of all-age worship, we are truly discipling each other and helping young and old into a mature faith that will last.

Thankfully, attitudes are slowly changing and it is encouraging that talk of death, in both secular and sacred settings, is becoming increasingly more common than it has been in the past. Bereavement support groups and 'death cafés' are being set up to address issues that formerly have been a social taboo. Even so, our new conversation places in the west have often been constructed with only a particular age group in mind – usually those who are older and for whom matters of life and death are looming larger. The fact that questions of death and dying can be relevant to people of all ages has been forgotten and needs to be recognised and recovered. It was there in the past when communities were smaller and more inward looking. Indeed, some cultures continue to function in an intergenerational way when it comes to talking about death, such as the all-age experience of the wake in Eire or family groups gathering in graveyards on 'the day of the dead' in Central America or the Far East.

The authors of this book are convinced that this all-age perspective is vital if we are to help each other talk about death and dying and face up to the big questions that these issues provoke. These are not just the concerns of older people but of the very young too, who ask the same questions but often in their own unique and sometimes very direct way. As Christian communities, we should not shy away from these conversations but provide opportunities to think these things through with each other – something that will grow both our own faith and the faith of those we talk with, from the youngest child to the most elderly great-grandparent.

Okay, we can begin to understand the importance of talking about death and dying intergenerationally, but where are the resources to do this well?

Well, this is exactly why we have put together this book!

Seriously Messy brings together Christian thinkers in the area of death and dying as well as those with a wide experience of intergenerational ministry to make such resources available. We planned the book carefully together but each wrote different parts and our individual stories and observations appear throughout. The book is in three parts. The opening chapters offer an easy-to-read overview of the issues of death and dying, and why this is such an important topic for churches. These chapters cover contemporary thinking and attitudes to the theme, and they unpack biblical references to death and dying. The case is made for the importance of shared conversations in this area between disciples of all ages, with practical suggestions as to how this can be done appropriately and sensitively when young and old are present. The important point is also made that many of us carry our own unresolved grief and questions in these areas, so we are making ourselves vulnerable when we enter into this sort of shared conversation. This is all the more reason to prepare well, and we urge readers not to skip the chapters in Part I before launching into the practical sessions. Leaders and Messy Church teams need to read these together and talk through what is being shared before they go on to listen to and come alongside those in their congregations.

Part II consists of a series of five short theological reflections. Traditional images and the language that Christians have always used when talking about death are explored. These five chapters are organised around the themes that form the basis for the practical sessions that follow in Part III, so it is a good idea to read the relevant one for the session you are planning. These themes are both natural and profoundly biblical:

- Remembering
- Saying goodbye and hello
- Sleeping tight
- Being loved
- Finding safe spaces

Each of the five Messy Church sections in Part III can be a stand-alone resource, offering material for a two-hour all-age service followed by a meal together. As with all traditional Messy Church sessions, there are ten activity ideas that prompt intergenerational conversations, as well as suggestions for a gathered time of interactive storytelling and prayer. At the end of the book is a list of further resources, which readers may want to follow up.

There is a huge wealth of material here for both Messy Church and traditional church leaders to use in a variety of settings. For example, many churches now hold annual bereavement services, where families come together to remember loved ones who have died. Material from this book will be helpful in this context, providing ideas for prayer stations, creative activities that can provide a focus for sensitive interactive worship, and stories from the Messy celebrations that can be woven into the liturgy. Similarly, hospital and hospice chaplains will also find resources to draw on when talking with families, particularly those facing the loss of a loved one. Working together on perhaps one carefully prepared activity from this book can help create a safe place for meaningful conversations to emerge and flourish. In this way, our hope is that the book will be widely used – not just in Messy Churches but wherever any church intentionally decides to bring together different generations to talk about what Christians believe about death. This is such an important but often marginalised dimension of our Christian discipleship.

Children are natural questioners – it is part of their spiritual nature and surely one of the reasons why Jesus offers them to us as model disciples. Among those questions will be those that relate to pain and suffering, death and what happens afterwards. For example, children very often ask questions about heaven, as all of you who work with children will have experienced! We shouldn't back away from these questions but be ready to talk about them with children, not as those who have all the answers but as fellow seekers, prepared to acknowledge our uncertainties and questions honestly. As we do this together, we will discover, as did the two disciples on the road to Emmaus, that Jesus will come and walk alongside us, to help us understand the mysteries of life, death and resurrection.

We offer you this book with the prayer that it will help resource shared conversations between young and old about the things that matter, enabling all of us to grow into mature followers of Jesus Christ, who said, 'I am the resurrection and the life' (John 11:25).

Part I

Death and dying

1

Death and life are messy

Messy beginnings and endings

The beginning of life and the end of life have much in common; one thing is their sheer messiness. And they are messy in more ways than one. First (and how we hate this), there are a lot of bodily fluids involved, ranging from sticky mess, through seeping mess, to full on fountains, each with its distinctive odour. In the gospel of John, we are told about some of Jesus' bodily fluids at the time of his death; a soldier pierced his side and 'blood and water came out' (John 19:34).

But there are other sorts of mess (and we don't much like these either). The course of labour is notoriously unpredictable and unique for every birth. The midwife tells you that you are on track to push the baby out in two hours, and six hours later you are still in the delivery room wondering why you didn't ask for an epidural. You are called to the deathbed of your granny only to find that she rallies, and you are filled with a messy mixture of relief and irritation that she didn't comply tidily with the doctors' pronouncements, and are then overwhelmed with guilt at such terrible thoughts. Older people near the end of life themselves often describe embarrassment at not shuffling off the mortal coil in a tidier fashion – of following a messy 'death trajectory'; they can see it as a kind of inconsiderateness on their part.

Birth and death are also messy in the sense that they are thresholds between one way of being and another. They are strange places where the normal rules of life dramatically break down. They can be places of deep physical intimacy, but they may also call up a sense of awe and wonder. Here, the life force that is simmering away on the back-burner in our normal daily routine suddenly bubbles up and boils over, and we are confronted with the fact that we are part of something much bigger.

One young couple rang up their local church to ask for a service of thanksgiving for the gift of their newborn son. 'We aren't religious,' the mum said. 'We just needed some way of saying "Thank you" and "Help!", and I walked past the church and thought that's a big building – like the bigness of what's just happened to us.'

Managing the mess

It's natural and right for us to want to manage mess, to bathe that newborn baby, to wash the recently deceased. After the birth of Jesus, we are told that his parents took him to the temple in Jerusalem. He had been circumcised at eight days old, but the temple visit was so that the mess of the birth could be managed. After 33 days, Mary could be declared mess-free through the offering of a sacrifice (Luke 2:22–24). And of course, after his very messy death, people tried to tidy Jesus up by wrapping him in cloths and laying him in a clean stone tomb, just as his mother had tidied him up as a newborn by wrapping him in cloths and laying him in a stone feeding-trough. The women who came to the tomb on the first Easter morning were there with the intent of embalming Jesus' body – literally 'fixing' him as best they could – but their plans got messed up.

In matters of life and death, it's wise to do some advance planning – to attend antenatal classes, to draw up a birth plan and, at the other end of life, to make a will and to set down our wishes for our medical and nursing care in our final days – though our actual control over these things may be less than we might like to think: 'the best-laid plans of mice and men...'

Another way that we manage the mess of thresholds – those ambiguous and mysterious places – is to bring family and friends of all generations together for a big party. It's telling that Mary and Joseph's visit to the temple becomes a cause of joy and celebration for two older people, Simeon and Anna. They make meaning by placing the event in a bigger picture, a wider story, and they offer words of wisdom and advice to the young couple. For ourselves, it is impossible to think of a Christening or a funeral without the 'do' or the wake that goes with it. These are occasions when family members, old and young, are reunited for a while, almost like a tribe, to say, 'Yes, this is us, we're still here!', before scattering back to the different parts of the country and wider world in which they spend their normal daily lives. There's something about managing mess that is also about remembering where we came from and where we belong.

But sometimes, instead of managing the mess, we try to pretend it doesn't exist. That is never a good idea. Perhaps we do this because we feel that mess might turn into chaos, might unleash forces that could overwhelm us. Many people today lead increasingly chaotic and unstable lives, both inside their heads and in their relationships, with little in the way of emotional or moral landmarks to hold and guide them. Chaos is indeed frightening. If we mistake mess for chaos, we will try to sweep it under the carpet, put the lid on it, refuse to tolerate it or even mention it, keep messy things separate and assign them to special places to be looked after by specialists.

But mess and chaos are not the same thing. Often, over-tidiness can be a sign of a deeper chaos. Life is messy, and that very messiness can be the seedbed of creativity and hope. A recent newspaper headline ran, 'Messy desks could be a sign of genius, say researchers.'[2]

Death is part of life

We are all familiar with nativity plays in which Mary and Joseph trudge from hotel to hotel, only to be told that they are fully booked until one innkeeper gives them room in his stable. But the actual story may have been a bit different. The Bible doesn't talk about stables at all, and the word traditionally translated 'inn' probably just means 'house'. In those days, if you went into labour, you did it in the communal living space, perhaps behind a curtain. Mary and Joseph were staying with relatives; the house was jam-packed (rather as ours might be at Christmas), so to get a bit of space and privacy they went downstairs, which is where the animals were also housed. The point is that birth happened in the thick of things. There was no way that it could be assigned to specialists in special places.

Until quite recently, it's been the same with death. It happened at home as part of the life of the household, not in a distant hospice, nursing home or hospital. The funeral took place in a church that was in the centre of the community, with business around carrying on pretty much as usual, with perhaps a pause for reflection and respect, not in an out-of-town crematorium. The deceased was buried in the churchyard, not a municipal cemetery. The managing of the mess was visible and present in the midst of normal life.

For the most part, this has now changed, and the business of death has been separated from life. In particular, we try to keep it hidden from children. Yet it is impossible to avoid it. Part of its messiness is that it breaks in and upsets out plans – plans for today, tomorrow, for the years ahead. We encounter it all around us: as children, we find that our beloved pets have limited lifespans; we cannot avoid bereavement, often beginning in childhood with the loss of a grandparent; violent death is all over the news and social media; we see the signs of our own mortality as our bodies change and age, no matter how fit we are or how much moisturiser we slap on.

This book is about lifting the lid on the messiness that is death, so that we can engage with it in a healthy way across the whole church family. This is about remembering and reclaiming something we have partly forgotten about the Christian story. At its centre is the idea that death is messy in the good way that leads to abundant life, not chaotic in the way that leads to drowning in eternal darkness.

The whole Christian story is about God's intentional messing up of the boxes we would put things in or the plans we would make. When 'the Word became flesh and pitched his tent among us'[3] uninvited, God had refused to stay in his heavenly box. What's more, he got his hands dirty with human life. This disturbed us so much that we sent him to his death – tidied away outside the city wall. But he messed that up too by breaking out of the tomb, a place where we had literally put the lid on him. He went through the messiness of birth, life and death, and he messed it about, turning it on its head so that we need not be afraid ever again.

But we still lose loved ones, we still grieve and we still fear death. We'll never bring together the two realities of the good news of our faith and our own experiences of living with bad news if we don't talk about it. The next chapters look at why we find this so difficult, how we might begin to do it, and how we can do it wisely and safely with the whole family of the church.

2

We need to talk about death

It's hard to talk about death

Chapter 1 talked about the messiness of birth and death and how those profound times of transition in life can challenge our attempts to manage and control them in our own way. Many people have very busy lives with schedules and appointments to keep, and from day to day we think we are in control of what happens in our lives – well, most of the time! Recently, I met a very busy person who seemed to be quite upset. When I asked if they were all right, they told me that for some reason they couldn't access their electronic diary and therefore had no idea what they were supposed to be doing that day. This left them feeling anxious and out of control. This was a small experience of how hard it can be when our everyday life is unexpectedly disrupted. We can all think of times in our own lives when things haven't gone to plan – our travel has been disrupted by strikes or bad weather, our purse or wallet has been stolen, we've fallen ill or we've been made redundant. These sorts of things force us to face up to the fact that we are not in control as much as we thought.

It's not surprising, therefore, that we find it hard to talk about death (the Great Disrupter) and even harder to think about it – not only does it mess with the everyday rhythm of our lives, but it is also fundamentally uncontrollable and unpredictable. This seems to be a particular problem in the 'developed' world: in the majority of world cultures, the reality of death has always been an openly acknowledged part of everyday life, and not just because life expectancies are low. In the industrialised west, we seem to have a strong need to be in control, and perhaps this is why most of us try not to think about death unless we run into it in some way (or it runs into us).

There are several other reasons why it is difficult for us to talk and think about death. It involves (unknown and possibly extreme) degrees of physical pain and discomfort; it separates loved ones; it is undergone alone; it interrupts our plans and projects and may make life seem pointless; and it seems to wipe out the person concerned.

It's good and healthy to talk about death and dying

However, death is part of life and the natural order, and we can't deal with it by avoiding it forever – at the back of our minds, we all know that we are going to have to face it for ourselves one day. It's good and healthy to be able to talk about it as a society and as individuals, and secular society is beginning to wake up to that fact. People are beginning to realise that, given our ageing population, as a society we can no longer brush death and all that is related to it under the carpet; we need to be able to talk about how we care for people who are dying, how we want our loved ones to be cared for and how we want to be cared for ourselves. I heard two women on a bus talking about their 'bucket lists' the other day and a couple in a café on holiday talking about the music they would like at their funeral.

'Death cafés', where people can come together to talk about death and dying over a coffee, are commonplace, and organisations such as the National Council for Palliative Care[4] and Dying Matters[5] have brought the topic of death and the process of dying back into the public arena. Dying Matters aims to help people talk more openly about dying, death and bereavement and to make plans for the end of life. The media are also playing their part, most recently through the work of Rachael Bland.[6]

All this is part of the widespread recognition that we do need to talk about death. If we at the very least do this, it means that we can be better prepared practically. But it will also help us face up to it psychologically; familiarity reduces anxiety and we can learn to manage the fear through play, humour, stories and films. We're all familiar with the gallows humour of people who work with death and tragedy, portrayed in detective stories and TV police series, and there are thousands of jokes about death, such as: Q. What's the definition of death? A. When you stop paying taxes suddenly; or: Q. Why do cemeteries have fences around them? A. Because people are dying to get in. Recall also the scary folk stories, such as Hansel and Gretel, in which Hansel is fattened up for the cooking pot by a cannibalistic witch – a pretty horrible prospect of death! The children manage to escape the witch (phew, what a relief!), but through these kinds of stories, generations of children have become familiar with the threat of death and learned to manage some of their fear.

Finally, talking and thinking a bit more about death can make us more mature human beings who have a better chance of living life well and wisely, because we will have seen the bigger picture and gained a sense of perspective and got our priorities straight.

Recall that getting involved with the mess of death is not the same as allowing ourselves to be engulfed in chaos. As we saw in chapter 1, we can and do find all sorts of creative ways in which to manage the mess.

Death is not the end

Right from the beginning, Christian communities have talked about and questioned the meaning, mystery and messiness of the death of Jesus and its significance for their lives. In his first letter to the Christians in Corinth, the apostle Paul responds to their questions and assures them, and us, that as Christians we need not be afraid of death. Yes, we will all die. Yes, our death may be deeply unpleasant, perhaps even agonising, but ultimately it cannot destroy us because through his death and resurrection, Christ has won the victory over death:

> 'Where, O death, is your victory? Where, O death, is your sting?'... But thanks be to God, who gives us the victory through our Lord Jesus Christ.
>
> 1 CORINTHIANS 15:55, 57

This gospel was liberating for the first Christian communities, which had a large proportion of slaves and occupied peoples as their members. These people were kept enslaved by the fear of death, the ultimate sanction of being killed by their masters and oppressors. But once you realise that death is not the end, you are liberated from this slavery – there is nothing that your oppressors can do to you. That's what turning the other cheek is about: 'Do not fear those who kill the body, and after that have no more that they can do' (Luke 12:4, RSV). Jesus showed himself victorious over the worst death possible, the one that was meant as a deterrent to keep the population cowed and subservient (Hebrews 2:14–15). Through history, this has offered people who have no options an option. Facing up to death doesn't just improve your well-being and make you wise; more fundamentally, it liberates you from the tyranny of fear. If the man pointing the gun at you can't make you do what he wants, you are free.

We need to include children in talk about death

Talking with a group of volunteers in a hospice, a woman in her 30s said that she had a real regret. Her grandma, whom she loved very much, died when she was six. With the best of intentions, her parents took her to stay with a friend while the funeral was taking place as they thought it would upset her too much to be there. The volunteer said she still felt that she never had the chance to say goodbye as she had wished, and that there was something unfinished. Her parents had tried to shield her from having to encounter death, but this had been neither possible nor helpful. The little girl had known that her grandma had died and had needed to say her own goodbye and to express her feelings for the person she loved.

We need to include children in our talk about death because they will encounter it anyway, because they are increasingly exposed to unreal images of death through electronic media, and because they need to be equipped with good information. Children may come across death in the loss of a pet or grandparent, or even a parent, sibling or friend. In some communities, there are high levels of violence; death or the threat of death are constantly in the air. Or there may be a disaster, as with Grenfell Tower in London, where communities are suddenly confronted with the violent death of many people of all ages. On the other hand, children are increasingly exposed to images of actual or fictional death in unreal or disembodied ways in video games, on television news or on social media. So there is a danger that the physical reality of death will be totally unexpected, shocking and confusing when they encounter it. It is better to put some wise resources in place than to leave children to face this subject uninformed (as was the case with sex in previous generations).

Dying Matters has recognised that schools are often unsure how to best support pupils who are affected by death and has called for dying, death and bereavement to be added to the national curriculum for secondary schools. Their chief executive has said, 'In order to break down taboos around death society-wide, it is vital that people of all ages feel supported to discuss their feelings around death and dying openly.'[7] St Christopher's Hospice in London is one example of an organisation that is helping children to do this; their Schools Project encourages children from both primary and secondary schools to work on creative projects alongside hospice patients.[8] Here, death is not brushed under the carpet, but is acknowledged as an inevitable part of life.

Of course, the resources we provide and the ways in which we talk about death must be appropriate to a child's age and developmental phase. We need to be careful about *how* we talk about death (see chapter 5), but if we can support one another in talking about it, we can be better prepared to meet it when we encounter it in our own lives, as we are sure to do.

By talking about it, we can begin to make sense of our experiences of death, dying and loss in the context of the good news of our faith as Christians, which is what the next chapter will explore.

3

We need to talk about death in church

Death is at the centre of our faith story

Those who meet together as church can't help but be aware that our whole faith story is based on death and life. This is the rhythm of the natural world: what is born will inevitably die as the generations succeed one another. In the context of faith, however, we experience a different gracious dynamic: through the story of salvation in the life, death and resurrection of Jesus, we see being revealed a deep structure of transformation. At the centre of this is the motif of the cross: the place where it looked like death had destroyed love became the place of triumph over death, offering the hope and promise of new and eternal life.

This story of the transformation of death to life is *the* great story at the centre of the Christian faith. It is the story that we tell day by day and week by week in our prayers, creeds, Bible readings and Holy Communion. It is the story that each one of us is part of as beloved children of God, to whom God has given the Spirit (2 Corinthians 5:4–5). In the daily humdrum of life, it may be that sometimes we lose sight of what a powerful and amazing story this is at work in our lives; that's why many churches have times in the church year when we can focus on the dynamic of death and resurrection. This happens in seasons such as Easter and at the time of All Souls and All Saints, when we remember loved ones who have died and all those who have gone before us.

But it is not only in our church worship that we constantly remember death and life; our church buildings themselves remind us of mortality. Older churches are full of memorials to the dead, both inside and out, and the architecture of churches themselves, built in the form of a cross, reminds us of the centrality of death in our faith story.

Research on talking about death in church

It's odd that even though we are constantly reminded about the pivotal role that death plays in the story of our faith, we don't seem to be very good at talking in church about the meaning of death for our lives and faith. We found in our research that when churches put on courses that provided opportunities for people to talk together about death and dying, there was a very positive response; people wanted to be able to talk about this profoundly important aspect of life, and it was a relief for them to have a safe and comfortable space in which to do this. One leader said, 'What struck me about it was just how eager people were… so many people came.' He learned 'about people's longing to know about it and their willingness to engage with it and not to be afraid of engaging people with it'. What's more, these were people who were regular churchgoers. Some of them remarked that they didn't get a chance to talk *properly* about these things in the rest of their church life.[9]

It's a relief to be able to reflect on death and life with others because, as one person said, 'there's still a huge reluctance with people to talk about death'. For some people, it can be difficult to open conversations about it with family and those who are closest to them, and so it can be helpful to be able to do that in the context of their faith community. If we can talk about it in church as a central part of our faith story, it is likely to make it easier for people to reflect on these issues together as part of the journey of faith. It's important that we have opportunities to reflect on our mortality, not only because people want and need to talk about death but also because knowing that we are not going to live on this earth forever focuses our attention on how to live our lives well. Reflecting on death moves us to consider more deeply our values, what really matters in life and what we believe about death and whatever comes next.

One course participant who was a regular member of a congregation spoke about how enriching it was to be able to talk with others with similar concerns. She realised that she was not alone with her concerns, questions and fears, but that other people were dealing with the same things. This enabled her to connect with people in a much deeper way than ever before, and she felt supported and much less isolated.

Being able to talk about death in church can be transformative for leaders too. One course leader found that in taking time to listen to people's stories and experiences, he learned new things about congregation members who had been coming to church for years. He also gained 'extraordinary insights that you're so grateful for', the opportunity to develop deeper pastoral relationships and food for reflection on faith and spirituality.

The elephant in the room

We have seen that when we do talk about death in church, it may be messy and challenging, but it can be one of the most enriching and creative things that we can do. It's central to our faith and, of course, in the end it cannot be avoided because one way or another, we all have to encounter death for ourselves. This is not to say that it is easy, and we may find it especially hard in the context of ministry with children and families. For example, it's a big challenge to put together Good Friday worship for children, and Easter has become synonymous with chocolate for most families. But if we have 'ears to hear' (Luke 8:8), we find that the Bible is full of stories of death and violence, all the way through. It's just that in telling the familiar stories, we tend to close our ears and tune out the menace of mortality that runs through everything just as it runs through our human lives.

Recall, for example, the story of Noah, where we focus on the animals that went into the ark two by two. Noah's arks are favourite toys for small children. Yet this is a story of a tsunami that devastated all living things 'that moved on the earth' (Genesis 7:21). We filter out the horror and the hard questions that come with this.

Again, think about the parting of the Red Sea to allow the Israelites to escape the Egyptians, which involves the death of a whole army (Exodus 14); the flight of Jesus' family into Egypt to avoid his being murdered by Herod and Herod's killing of male babies around Bethlehem in revenge for being thwarted (Matthew 2:13–18); Simeon's calm acceptance that he is ready to die, having seen the Christ (Luke 2:29–32); the parable of the good Samaritan, where a man is attacked and left 'half dead' with his life in the balance (Luke 10:29–37); Herod's cruel and grotesque beheading of John the Baptist, in which John's head is offered on a dish to Herodias' daughter to please her (Matthew 14:3–12); the death and restoration of the son of the widow of Nain (Luke 7:11–15). Once you have your antennae tuned to the threat of mortality, the list of stories in which its presence is central and inescapable is endless!

Yet our instinct is to protect children (and perhaps ourselves) from such things. This is misguided. In one of her books on childhood, Sally Goddard Blythe writes that death is now 'sanitised' because natural events have become:

> ... hidden away in hospitals, abattoirs, nursing homes, morgues and chapels of rest... If as parents we seek to protect our children from all unpleasant events we do not equip them to deal with the real world.[10]

She goes on to say that, as we've already noted, traditional fairy tales (with all their violence) have the potential to help children process their emotions and to face the fact that life is not happy all the time. Fairy tales are fantasies, but they can be full of truth. We need to rediscover this aspect of our own story, that of God's dealings with his people, a real story that is full of *the* truth.

A matter of death and life

We know from our own and others' experience, from what we see in the media and from the Bible that people of any age may experience death and loss. Because of this, it is important that we are able to talk about it together and, in so doing, to support and equip people for whenever they encounter mortality in their own lives. We need a more intentional and imaginative approach to help people explore this central aspect of life and stop it being the elephant in the room.

This is an area where there will be loads of questions, especially maybe for unchurched people – and that is good. We need to give people the chance to explore this unfamiliar ground and to ask their questions. For churched people, there is a need to be able to embrace more fully and authentically the joy of the resurrection, even in hard times and challenging situations. For everyone who engages with this, there is the opportunity to learn about life from the perspective of death.

There are lots of different ways in which you can help people to do this. For example, the Church of England has produced Gravetalk cards[11] to help people open up conversations about death, and we have produced a multimedia resource called Death and Life.[12] But this book is about exploring mortality with the whole family across the generations, and we explore this in the next chapter.

4

We need to talk about death with the whole church family

Church at its best is one of the few social gatherings where you can find representatives from every age of life, from the babe in arms to a nonagenarian in a wheelchair. A healthy church community is surely one which embraces all-age diversity and celebrates God-given difference, where there is a dynamic encounter of like with unlike. The perspectives of someone who has lived through war in the last century or the sexual revolution of the 1960s, alongside a young person who is a 21st-century digital native, may be very different, but each needs the other to enrich lives for good and most assuredly for growing in faith.[13]

One of the great things about Messy Church is that it sets up the conditions not just to bring the different generations together in one place but also to support fruitful encounters between them.

'Old and young together!'[14]

There will be representatives of several generations in a church, not just the very old and very young but everyone in between. But perhaps it is the oldest old (folk in their 80s) who may have most to offer the rest of the church family on the subject of death. For a start, they are the closest to death. But just as important, it is this older generation that understandably has the most interest in death and dying and is most likely to have reflected deeply on it.

Death is part of life; from the day we are born, we are dying. Parts of our body are dead and can be discarded. Cutting nails and hair is something that intrigues young children. 'Why doesn't it hurt?' they ask; 'Because that part is dead,' we reply. This invites the unspoken thought, 'My whole body will be like that one day; nothing will hurt it any more...'

Yet in our youth, our bodies are wondrous things that grow and become stronger and more capable every day. It's when children look at the bodies of older adults that they get an inkling of the fact that, like the heavens, we 'will all wear out like a garment' (Psalm 102:26). Of course, the middle-aged know this only too well and either try to avoid thinking about it or actively take steps to stave it off. There is then nothing quite like the shock of receiving an over-50s magazine or a Senior Railcard: 'Surely there must be some mistake?'

This is one reason some of us avoid older people. They remind us that we too are wearing out and that one day we will die. But young children aren't threatened and repelled by wrinkled bodies, age spots on hands, hairy nostrils, dentures, spectacles or walking sticks in the way that adults are. They can be fascinated by them and by the difference between these and their own fresh skin, sharp eyes and sturdy limbs. Talking about these differences, exploring the beauty and resilience of elderly bodies and the stories behind callouses, scars or imperfectly set bones, can help all of us to understand the whole sweep of a person's life and the way that history is written on the body.

It also puts us in touch with the fact that death is a physical process with its own bodily changes. When an elderly woman died, her small grandson was fascinated by the fact that in her last days her fingers had gradually turned blue. 'Would Granny still be alive if they cut her fingers off?' he asked. Sadly, nobody replied. Talking about the physical reality of ageing in life can prepare us to talk about the physical reality of death.

'Some things that should not have been forgotten were lost'[15]

People from older generations will remember rituals around death that may have been all but forgotten by present generations. They are more likely to have seen the body of a dead person or attended a funeral with an open coffin (a practice still common in some cultures today). They may be able to bear witness to practices such as stopping and bowing or removing the hat when a funeral cortège goes by, or drawing all the curtains in the home when someone has died. These are all marks of respect both for the individual concerned and the great mystery of death itself; the idea of 'respect' can form the focus for some helpful conversations. How would we show respect today? Why do we feel the need to show it at all? What exactly is respect?

There is also a wisdom that can come with length of years. Encountering someone who has learned to live well with solitude and frailty can make these things much less frightening, and there may be tips to be gained. Research suggests that learning to enjoy one's own company, to savour the moment and to delight in small things are skills that need to be learned early if they are to help us age well.[16]

Knowing how to say goodbye

For many children and young people, the first major loss they experience is that of a grandparent. My grandmother died when I was 10 and she was 73. She had inoperable cancer, so she knew it was coming. Unbeknown to my parents, we had several conversations in which she tried to prepare me for her departure. Without ever mentioning the word 'death', she told me that she was very sad that she would not see me grow to adulthood, but that she was in a lot of pain and was going to a lovely garden where she would feel well again. She would look down from that place and follow my life with interest. Above all, if I ever got into trouble, I was to remember that she would always be with me.

Those conversations had a massive influence for good on my life. We need to set up conditions to make those sorts of conversations happen easily and naturally, not just in the case of terminal illness but in a lighter-touch, more general way between the generations. We need to be able to talk naturally about heaven, of our hope of going there, of the reality of parting, but also of continuing bonds between the departed and the living. The safest way to do this is in the context of something else, such as a craft activity – a gently playful, relaxed space. This might be the sort of space where a conversation between Granny and grandchild is overheard by Mum, who says nothing but receives a blessing from it. You can't force these things; they just happen if the setting is right.

'It is to such as these that the kingdom of heaven belongs'[17]

In some of our research, we asked older people to tell us their ideas about death. One idea that kept coming up was that dying is a bit like being born. One lady wrote:

> We enter this world as babies,
>   all unknowing,
>   but there are people waiting to care for us.
> Death is a similar 'door'.
> There will be care for us on the other side of this door too.

It's not just the young who benefit from being with the old. It can be a two-way street. There can be a special closeness between babies and those in their last years (as with Simeon and Anna). Somehow, the new little person reminds the one who is close to death that life goes on, but also rejuvenates them and gives them confidence and hope for their own rebirth.

The very young and the aged can also have a lot in common:

> Said the little boy, 'Sometimes I drop my spoon.'
> Said the old man, 'I do that, too.'
>
> The little boy whispered, 'I wet my pants.'
> 'I do that, too,' laughed the little old man.
>
> Said the little boy, 'I often cry.'
> The old man nodded. 'So do I.'
>
> 'But worst of all,' said the boy, 'it seems grown-ups don't pay attention to me.'
> And he felt the warmth of a wrinkled hand. 'I know what you mean,' said the little old man.[18]

Grieving together

Sometimes a death happens that affects the whole church community. It may be the sudden, unexpected death of a relatively young person who is well-known and well-loved, perhaps a leader in the church. The circumstances may be particularly distressing, as in the case of suicide (which is more common than we might think).

Assumptions about the way things are – plans and projects, ideas about God's providence – can all be thrown up in the air. A church community will respond best to this if it can talk and pray honestly about issues and feelings, and together make some meaning in the midst of loss and confusion. A culture in which talking about death has become a normal part of church life rather than an extraordinary response to a crisis will help this greatly. A culture in which the whole church family is involved will mean that all are included in the process of grieving, and that the 'grown-ups' actually do pay attention to everyone's needs. This is surely right, for:

If one member suffers, all suffer together with it; if one member is honoured, all rejoice together with it.

1 CORINTHIANS 12:26

5

Taking care when talking with children about death and loss

One reason we avoid talking with children about death is that we don't want to traumatise or inflict some permanent damage on them. If the children are not part of our family circle and we only meet them at church, and perhaps not often, then we will want to tread even more carefully.

This is a good instinct, but it doesn't mean that we can't mention death and dying at all. In this chapter, we offer some basic guidelines for doing it well.

Talk about life

The Messy Church sessions in this book are organised around themes that are about *living life* well: remembering, saying goodbye and hello, sleeping tight, being loved and finding safe spaces. All of these themes have an intense significance in the context of death, but because they also apply to life they help us to see death as a part of life. It would be possible to do the sessions without mentioning death directly at all, and the extent to which you talk about death in a full-frontal way will depend on your group and its needs and will be responsive to the questions that come up.

These sessions are not designed as bereavement counselling, but instead offer ways of putting a framework in place for people (adults and children) to make meaning in their own way and at their own pace. People make meaning in various ways. The most basic way is by sticking close to someone who seems to hold meaning and will just be there while we journey into challenging thought-places. Another way is through story; we might think of living the Christian life as a process in which God's story and our story come together. A third way is through creativity – artistry and craft. Here, we work out meaning through action and we may use symbols.

In his book *Godly Play: An imaginative approach to religious education*, Jerome Berryman tells the story of Bobby, a little boy who used story and symbol to make meaning, helped by the reliable presence of his trusted teacher. Bobby made several pictures of the mustard tree in Jesus' parable (Mark 4:30–32). Bobby returned to this topic over several weeks, focusing on the birds of the air that lived in the tree. These birds had taken on huge significance for him and, though it was never actually spoken of, it was clear that his artwork was helping him to engage with death:

> What is happening is... the raising of awareness that creating is a whole new way of being in the world, a way of being in the image of God, the Creator. When this experience is supported as it was for Bobby, even the threat of death and separation can be reframed so that one can 'fly away' to take up new challenges.[19]

In a similar way, these Messy Church sessions combine being with trusted people, hearing God's story and engaging with creative activities so that both adults and children, if they wish, may go about making meaning of life and death – but without rubbing their noses in it.

Be real about fear and really listen

Children are easily frightened, but part of the task of childhood is to be able to develop a tolerance of moderate degrees of fear. That's why children (to varying degrees, depending on their age and temperament) can be fascinated by danger, horror and violence; enjoy games that involve shock, screaming in a mix of pleasurable excitement and anxiety; and love roller-coaster rides. Where this is well supervised, guided and 'held' by trusted adult caregivers, it helps their development. Sometimes the excitement or fear can get a bit out of hand; there may be nightmares or other signs of anxiety for a day or two, but these usually settle quickly.[20]

Facing up to fear is good. Writing about this in the context of Halloween, Martyn Payne says:

> Banning things outright can often cause more problems than it solves. Having one evening a year on which some of the more uncomfortable dimensions of our lives, such as the fear of death and of the unknown, are brought out into the open to be laughed at and played with in a safe way can be very healthy, particularly for children...

> One of the positive outcomes of recent changes in our approach within children's ministry has been the realisation that we need to explore all aspects of our faith openly with children, listening carefully to their questions and answers as we accompany them on a spiritual journey of discovery, learning from and with them as we read Bible stories together.[21]

The Messy Church sessions in this book are in this spirit, and listening attentively to children's worries and questions is a crucial part of them. These sessions do not focus on Halloween itself, but of course you may decide to use one or more of them around that time.

Keep it real

We are all prone to turning processes into persons. Adults do this when they talk about 'Storm Emma' or 'The Grim Reaper', but children do it much more easily. Sometimes this is unhelpful. If we talk to them about 'death' or 'the dead', they are likely to see these as bogeymen who might be out to get them.

Instead, it is better to rob death of its sting by talking about *real* human beings (and animals) who die and by keeping fixed on the *real* human being – Jesus – who has defeated death.

Manage fears and anxieties: 'It's okay'

It is important to communicate to children that everything is fundamentally well with the world – that 'it's okay' – even if bad things happen to us or if we experience upsetting feelings. This is, after all, the message of the cross; God was there in Jesus, transforming the worst thing that could possibly have happened.

The idea that it's okay even if bad stuff happens is *not* the same as saying that bad stuff doesn't happen to Christians; it means that we believe that God is in charge and will ultimately turn things to good. The idea that it's okay even if we experience upsetting feelings is *not* the same as saying we shouldn't be upset; it means that we believe that God is with us in all our feelings, happy and sad.

There's a third okay to be communicated: 'It's okay not to have all the answers.' After all, even the apostle Paul describes this territory as 'a mystery' (1 Corinthians 15:51).

We generally communicate these ideas by our behaviour rather than in words: by not panicking or being fazed by bad stuff, but at the same time being prepared to name it as bad and not brushing it under the carpet; by showing empathy for distress, but gently drawing the distressed person back to a place of peace; by being confident to say, 'I don't know' or, 'I find that hard to understand too', yet holding fast to some heart-truths of our faith:

- God is love: God wants to give us our hearts' desire.
- God is with us through good and bad: God will never let us go.
- God is fair and knows each person's story; he is never cruel or unjust.
- It really *is* okay, because in Jesus, God has acted decisively to redeem the world.
- In taking human form as Jesus, God has shown how precious and important our bodies are.
- God delights in the whole of creation, not just human beings.

Reminding ourselves of these deep truths as we pray in preparation for a session will help us to provide what is technically called a 'holding environment', within which people of all ages can explore difficult feelings and ideas with a sense of basic security.

Take account of how children think about life and death

First idea: death as permanent separation

Preschool children appear to have little understanding of death, but by about five or six years of age children will know the word and understand that death is irreversible and that it happens to all living creatures. At this age, children's ideas of causation are not very developed. They understand death as something that is caused by external things such as poison, guns or 'bad people'. Crucially, they may wonder if they could cause a death by being naughty. It's good to be alert to this so that you can offer reassurance if a child brings it up.

Although children of this age understand that death is not the same as falling asleep or going away on holiday, they quite reasonably see death as a 'kind of' falling asleep forever or going away to a place that is too far away to come back from. They have grasped that they won't see the deceased again, and the sense of separation makes them sad (to varying degrees depending on the closeness of the relationship). At this age, they don't have a very developed understanding of what happens to the body of the deceased.

Second idea: death as the body stopping working

From about the age of seven, children begin to grasp the reality that death is actually going to happen personally to them and can't be avoided – it's not just something that affects old people. This is such an emotionally challenging idea (as it is for any of us) that they may simply prefer not to think about it; this should be respected.

Also from this age, children begin to understand more of how the body works and that there are different organs for breathing, pumping blood, thinking, digesting and so on. They begin to understand that if one or more of these vital organs stops working, the body will no longer function and will simply cease. So, as they begin to understand physical life better, they begin to see death as life coming to an end.

Seeing death as a biological reality in this way enriches children's overall understanding. It can make death less frightening because it is seen as a natural process. In session three, we explore the ideas that bodies can be transformed and that life goes on. It may be helpful as part of this session to start by asking any children (especially those under eight) a couple of questions to get a sense of their understanding of the body; for example, 'What is the heart for?', 'What happens if someone's heart stops beating?' and 'After someone has died, does their heart keep on beating?' This will help you gauge their level of understanding and give you an opportunity to explain some basics, if necessary.

Bringing the two ideas together

As adults, we are able to hold together the psychological reality of death (separation from our loved one) with the physical reality (her bodily decay). But we find it difficult. This is why seeing the coffin at a funeral can bring us up short (and it lies behind the increasing popularity of memorial services without the body of the deceased present).

This must be even more difficult for children, hence most experts think that using phrases like 'he's fallen asleep' or 'she's gone to a better place' is not helpful when explaining to a child that someone has died. It is always good to use clear and direct language to explain what is meant. The best way to talk about death is to use clear bodily language: 'Grandad's heart got weak and it couldn't keep him alive anymore.'

But – and this is a big but – children are a lot more sophisticated than we often give them credit for. Even from a young age, they know the difference between 'Grandad's fallen asleep' and 'Grandad has died. It's *like* when he used to go to sleep,' especially if we are careful with our use of language.

More than that, children are able to enter the zone of the imagination, something that has been described as the world of 'as if': 'It's *as if* Grandad has fallen asleep.' In the world of 'as if', play and symbols are important. I once watched a two-year-old with a new baby brother place a mummy and baby plastic horse in a play house and say, 'Where me?' before finding another horse to place with them. He didn't need to explain himself further. The same child had a real pet cat that he liked to feed; he found the suggestion of giving the same food to his beloved toy cat ridiculous. Even at this tender age, he was confident at inhabiting the world of imagination and not only knew the difference between this and the 'real' world, but also understood how the two worlds connect.

In a similar way, it seems that children can hold together the idea that they will never see a loved one again in this life with the notion that sometimes it's as if she were here with us. This is a particularly vivid kind of remembering, something we explore in session 1. But it can be more than that; many of us have had a sense of presence, dreams or even visions of deceased loved ones, and this can also be the experience of children. This is usually a normal, benign and comforting outworking of the 'as if' imagination (how often do we say on waking from a dream, 'It was *as if* it was really happening'?) – a part of healthy grieving, not a form of spiritual oppression or haunting. Sometimes a child will need to be reassured of this.

The bottom line: 'It's okay; I'm here'

The child's need for a secure sense of attachment to loving caregivers cannot be overstated. We can only face the challenges of this life and ultimately face up to death if we carry this into adulthood with us. The power of the gospel is its assurance that, even if human caregivers have let us down, God himself is with us as our loving parent, friend and champion. When the disciples were alone in their boat, almost overwhelmed by a storm, Jesus came to them saying, 'Take heart, it is I; do not be afraid' (Matthew 14:27), almost as we might say to a crying child, 'It's okay; I'm here.'

Of all the lessons that a child might take from these Messy Church sessions, the most important one is that God loves him or her unconditionally and will always be there for them. It is a key part of sessions 1, 2 and 4. Everything else rests on this. Everything that we do should point to this:

> Neither death, nor life, nor angels, nor rulers, nor things present, nor things to come, nor powers, nor height, nor depth, nor anything else in all creation, will be able to separate us from the love of God in Christ Jesus our Lord.
> ROMANS 8:38–39

6

We need to take care of ourselves

A palliative care consultant related how amused she was when, attending a general medical conference, she was asked by a colleague from a different specialty, 'What is your mortality rate?' She replied, 'One hundred per cent. Every patient I care for dies.' We need to take care of ourselves when helping people to reflect on death and dying, because our mortality is the one inescapable human reality that we all share. This can make working in this area messy, because when we reflect on it with others, at some level we are always aware that it will seep out and touch our own lives; we too will eventually die, and the issues that people raise may well also be ours. One group leader said, 'I'm on the same journey… It's not just me leading a group of others, but the same issues that I am inviting them to engage with, I engage with myself.'

This means that we are likely to be touched and affected by what adults and children share, often in ways and at times that we least expect, and which may take us by surprise in a messy way. To explore this area of life in a way that is safe for others and for ourselves, we therefore need to be prepared for thoughts, questions and feelings that may be raised for us. John's gospel describes the death of Lazarus, the friend whom Jesus loved. Jesus is moved in the depths of his humanity when he encounters the family and friends of the dead man grieving and weeping bitterly. While still on the outskirts of the village where they lived, Jesus had declared himself the source of eternal life, but when he draws near and encounters the rawness of human grief, things inevitably get messy; we are told twice that 'he was deeply moved in spirit and troubled' (John 11:33, RSV; see also 11:38). Jesus loved Lazarus and these people – of course he was moved by their grief and distress! Even though we may have the assurance of eternal life, there is no avoiding the messiness of being human.

Because we are likely to be touched and affected by what people share, it may be wise to think twice before getting involved with a Seriously Messy session if you have recently been bereaved. Of course, everyone is different and people cope with bereavement in different ways, but if you are freshly grieving, it may be a good idea to talk about your situation with someone who knows you well and can help you decide if it is the right time for you to get involved.

Although we can never be prepared for every eventuality, there are things we need to think about to ensure that we keep things as safe as possible both for ourselves and for those we work with. Taking care of ourselves is basic to this.

Be honest with yourself

Engaging with death, loss and our ultimate destiny throws a searchlight on what we really think, believe and feel – what really matters. It requires us to be true to ourselves and to what is in our hearts and minds; we need to be as honest as possible about our own attitude to death and our beliefs and doubts about what comes next. This may well be a bit messy too – and that's fine. Our attitude and beliefs may change over time as we go through different life phases and experiences and learn new things. It's honesty, together with trust in God, that matters. No human being has all the answers – so that's a relief! You are in good company with the apostle Paul when he writes in his letter to the Corinthians that it is only when we die that all will be revealed and we shall understand fully (1 Corinthians 13:12). At the heart of death and life lies a glorious mystery that human beings can't fully comprehend. What we do need to have is some genuine hope in the face of death and the capacity to be alongside people in their explorations and uncertainty. As we saw in chapter 5, it's okay not to have all the answers, okay to have difficult questions ourselves and okay to acknowledge the mystery at the heart of this life. Not everything can be fixed, and sometimes we need to live with questions. After all, this is a life of faith in the God of love, compassion and mercy, whose Son came that we may have abundant life (John 10:10).

It takes (at least) two

You will need help to run a session, so it is important that there is at least one other person with whom you can pray, plan the activities and lead. Usually, you will be part of a bigger team. Remember that Jesus recognised the need for mutual support when he sent the disciples out 'two by two' (Luke 10:1, RSV). Working with others you trust and feel comfortable with means that you can share questions, ideas and concerns and provide support for each other. The other advantage is that each of you will bring different perspectives, experiences and understandings to resource the session. It will also probably make the whole session a lot more relaxed – and more enjoyable too!

After the session, it is a good idea to reflect together on:

- how you think the session went in general
- how you felt about leading the session
- any significant questions or issues that emerged
- any follow-up with people who might be needed
- whether there is anything that you would do differently next time.

If something has unexpectedly been raised for you by what has been shared, this is also a time when you can acknowledge that. This time of reflection offers an opportunity not only for support and learning, but also a necessary space in which leaders can be accountable to one other. It may strike you as an added burden, but it is in fact time well spent. Which brings us to…

Take enough time

We all know how busy and pressured life can be. It is tempting to try to cram into our time as much as possible and to dash from one thing to the next, trying to achieve the maximum in the limited time available. But sometimes less is more. It can be helpful to recall the different approach that Jesus took. He could only carry out the work he had to do because he created space around his ministry. The gospels describe how he would often leave the crowds and go away to a solitary place to pray, reflect and be with God (e.g. Luke 6:12). Taking this time enabled him to stay rooted in God and in himself so that he could remain focused on the important work he needed to do.

Give yourself enough time: time to prepare the session and to reflect and pray in advance. You will also need to allow yourself time to process any challenging thoughts and feelings that are shared with you. If you have a conversation about death, don't immediately rush into the next thing you have to do; create some space around it and give yourself a moment to process what has been shared. Before or after a session, you might find it helpful to do something relaxing, such going for a walk, taking a bath or listening to music. Only you know what you need and what works for you; the important thing is to look after yourself as you journey alongside people who are reflecting on the messiness of human endings.

Taking care of ourselves and caring for others

Love your neighbour as yourself.
MATTHEW 22:39

It is generally accepted that caring for ourselves is fundamental to caring for others. For example, if we are tired and feel grumpy, or if we feel anxious and afraid, it is hard to give our full attention to the people for whom we care. The focus will be on ourselves rather than on the other person. I can't listen to someone's story if I'm falling asleep; all I'll probably be thinking about is how to get away and get some rest! So taking care of ourselves is not an optional extra but a serious responsibility and the foundation of any work we do with other people. We need to love and care for ourselves if we are to love and care for our neighbour.

The basic principles set out in this chapter should help you to:

- Be aware of what is going on in your own life.
- Be aware that you may be affected by what people share with you and that things may get messy.
- Work with supportive co-leaders so that you can reflect together and hold each other to account.
- Take enough time, create space around the work – and relax!

If we take care of ourselves, we will be able to run safe, enriching and creative sessions in the spirit of the great commandment that we should love our neighbour as ourselves.

Part II

Theological reflections

7

Remembering

Memories are made of this

How do we remember someone who has died? The most obvious way is to have a memorial service or event. These days, funerals have become at least as much about remembering the deceased as about dispatching his or her remains. There is often a photograph of the person, perhaps in younger days or happier times, on the service sheet; if the service is in a church, the sermon takes a back seat to the sharing of memories by friends and family, often in the form of a life story or the retelling of an incident that seems to sum the person up; the deceased is laid to rest in a place that is marked in some way as a memorial. We do this for our loved ones and we do this as a nation for our service people on Remembrance Sunday.

But it doesn't stop there. We remember, and often keep special, the day of birth and the day of death of our loved ones. We treasure the possessions they have left to us. It can take parents by surprise when their sophisticated adult children insist on keeping worthless items left in a deceased grandparent's home – a moth-eaten troll, a decrepit Monopoly game, a certain cup or plate, a penknife. These can be precious emblems of things they are in danger of forgetting: times of innocence and magical wonder from their childhood, a sense of security in a wide family circle, a grandparent who was previously a fit and trusted older companion rather than a frail invalid.

If we have been left money, we want to use it wisely, but we also want to use it in a way that fits the character and personality of the one we have lost. My mum was always disappointed with my penchant for charity shop clothing. I spent the small amount she left me on a brand new cashmere coat. Every time I wear it, I think of her and imagine that she would approve.

If there is enough money, we might choose to set up a fund in our loved one's name. But even if there is no money, we try to live our lives as they would have wanted. This can emerge in unexpected ways: a teenager once said she wasn't going to go along with her friends in some escapade because 'Grandma would have said it was cheap.' If you ask young couples who bring infants to church for baptism or dedication about the names they have chosen for their babies, there is, more often than not, at least one that belonged to a deceased beloved relative; and if you ask young couples who don't often come to church why they have chosen a church wedding, 'Granny would have wanted it' is a frequent reply. To use a phrase of Jesus, they are doing it 'in remembrance of her' (Mark 14:9).

'Remember me'

Remembering plays a central role in the life of faith too. Right through the Old Testament, God keeps reminding his people to remember him, and in particular to remember what sort of God he is – the one who brought them safely out of Egypt against all the odds (Deuteronomy 5:15), who is true to himself, who has saved and who can be trusted to keep on saving. People are sometimes told to remember how God acted in the history of Israel (Isaiah 46:3–4; Psalm 78); at other times it's more personal: individuals remember how God has acted at key moments in their lives and this gives them hope for the future (Psalm 71:17–20).

God himself also promises to remember. In fact the relationship between God and his people seems to be one of *mutual remembering*. This is the nature of the covenant: God sustains people by keeping them in mind; they in turn remember him by trusting him enough to turn to him and by keeping his commandments. And it all seems to be focused on having a meal – the Passover.

This carries on into the New Testament. Jesus tells us that the prodigal son remembered – he remembered that there was 'bread enough and to spare' in his father's house (Luke 15:17), so he turned around with the intent of seeking his father and committing to live in the way his father would want. But the father had never forgotten his wayward son – he was on the lookout for him. So it was *mutual remembering*. We could also think of this as re-membering, a reconstruction of the son and of the relationship. And of course it all ends in a wonderful feast – the equivalent of a hog roast – which took place because 'this son of mine was dead and is alive again' (Luke 15:24).

Remembering, then, seems to be a matter of life and death; it seems to involve doing, not just thinking; it seems to be central to relationship; and in some mysterious way it's all bound up with eating.

After all, it wouldn't be a funeral without a wake.

'I love you'

'I love you father and mother and Toy. If we can get out, please can you take me to eat at a pan-fried pork restaurant? I love you.'[22]

These were words written by one of the boys trapped in the Tham Luang caves in Thailand in July 2018. Of course, here the mention of food is no mystery: he must have been starving! But his message of love is typical of those sent by people who think they are about to be separated from loved ones by death. It has been said that for adults these messages boil down to two statements: 'I love you' and 'Look after the others.'[23]

This is so very like Jesus' long goodbye to his friends as recorded in John 13—18. Again and again, he tells his disciples that he loves them; he also tells them to look after each other by washing each other's feet. And it all happens 'during supper' (John 13:2).

The other gospels tell us that Jesus understood the supper in itself to be a way of remembering him. He was troubled and distressed during the meal, yet he had also longed to eat it with his friends. We call that meal 'the last supper', which implies that there were lots of suppers that went before it. Sharing bread with others was a Jesus kind of thing; it's how he was recognised at the inn at Emmaus and on the lakeshore over breakfast. He asked us to remember him whenever we bless, break and share his bread and his story. He didn't just want us to remember his teachings; he also wanted us to remember *him*, a real flesh-and-blood human being. He didn't just want us to remember him in our minds, but also to remember him with our bodies through the action of eating. He didn't just want us to remember his life with gratitude, but he also wanted us to grasp the violent reality of his death in the torn bread and the bloody wine. Above all, he wanted us to be transformed and made fully alive through the bittersweet experience of remembering, to be reminded that he has conquered death, to be remade out of our brokenness into his body.

> The cup of blessing that we bless, is it not a sharing in the blood of Christ? The bread that we break, is it not a sharing in the body of Christ? Because there is one bread, we who are many are one body, for we all partake of the one bread.
> 1 CORINTHIANS 10:16–17

Crafting memories, remaking people

So, in our remembering of others who are no longer with us, and in our desire to be remembered by others, we are close to the centre of our faith. Psychologists tell us that remembering is not like replaying a film – it's a creative act of reconstruction. It's also something we do together, each of us adding details others might have forgotten. It may make us cry; more often it will make us smile, perhaps even laugh.

It is frequently observed that a funeral is where you find out things about the deceased that you didn't know before. That's because people are multifaceted and their friends, colleagues and family will see different facets. We need more than one story to do justice to a person (that's one reason we have four gospels). Collective and cooperative remembering is a way in which the deceased is re-membered and made more real, and it also draws those who remember closer together.

People who are bereaved say that the greatest comfort they receive from others comes not from expressions of sympathy but from reminiscences about the one they have lost. It assures them that they didn't just imagine their loved one. Expressing memories tells others that the person has made their mark on our lives, and it confirms that he or she really did walk this earth.

Memory is a gift from God, and when we remember we are joining with God's life-giving work.

8

Saying goodbye and hello

'Parting is such sweet sorrow'

We have all had the bittersweet experience of having to say goodbye to someone that we love. Perhaps you've had to say goodbye to family or friends after a visit you've enjoyed so much that you don't want it to end, or perhaps a close friend has moved away and you miss the laughter and shared times that you took for granted, never imagining that the companionship would end.

One of the most poignant moments can be waving someone off on a long journey at a railway station or airport. There can be a mixture of emotions: perhaps excitement and happiness for them, knowing that they are going to have new experiences to enjoy, but for a brief moment, as they disappear from sight and we are left standing on the platform before we return to our familiar daily life, there may also be feelings of emptiness and sadness. They have gone away and, although we are certain that we will see them again, still, we have to carry on our lives without them being around as usual; we miss them and look forward to seeing them again. Rather than 'goodbye', perhaps the French phrase 'au revoir' – 'until I see you again' – is more accurate.

Shakespeare captured brilliantly the 'sweet sorrow' of two young people in love having to say goodbye in his play *Romeo and Juliet*. Many of us probably know the phrase even if we're not aware of where it comes from. He captures the moment when they have to say goodbye after their first real meeting; they are so bound up with each other that they can hardly bear to be parted, even though they know that they will see each other again. In that intense moment of anticipated separation, it feels to them as though they will not be able to tolerate, or perhaps even survive, being apart from one another. At the heart of this bittersweet moment, there is a paradox: it is only because their experience of first love is so intense that they are so sad to be parting – the measure of their love is the measure of their sadness at being apart. The pain of loss is the other side of loving.

Feeling sad is a natural and inevitable part of having to say goodbye to someone we love who has died, or having to let go of the people, places or ways of life that we would like to hold on to. But it may be mixed with feelings of relief that their suffering is over, or satisfaction that they lived a full life and died a dignified death. This bittersweet mix of feelings tells us that, sad as it can be, there are times when we need to say goodbye so that new life can grow and develop, part of the natural process of life and death: 'For everything there is a season... a time to be born, and a time to die' (Ecclesiastes 3:1–2).

'Love is strong as death'[24]

When someone we love dies, we can feel deep pain and sadness at having to say goodbye. At times, we might feel that being separated from them is almost unbearable. But somewhere deep down, we also know that the sadness is the other side of the love that we hold in our hearts. The one thing that doesn't change or diminish is that love that we share.

We can usually tolerate the 'goodbye' – or is it 'au revoir'? – with the love and support of those who care for us, because we know in our heart of hearts that the love we shared when they were alive will always remain and that nothing – certainly not death – can take that away.

The Bible assures us that the strength and power of love is stronger than anything, because love comes from God and, indeed, God is love (1 John 4:8). It is out of love that God created us, and God calls each one of us by name (Isaiah 43:1). So, although we may have to say goodbyes in our lives, and we may sometimes feel overwhelmed by waves of sadness, God's love is there to sustain us, and we are given the promise:

> When you pass through the waters, I will be with you; and through the rivers, they shall not overwhelm you.
> ISAIAH 43:2

'Many waters cannot quench love'

In the Bible, many stories of goodbye and hello involve water, and in particular having to cross through or over this dangerous, turbulent element. Rivers, lakes and seas separate one person from another, just as the River Jordan separated God's people from the promised land. Yet we are assured that, however turbulent the crossing, 'many waters cannot quench love, neither can floods drown it' (Song of Songs 8:7).

Traditionally, rivers mark boundaries between where we are now and the promise of new life and unexplored territory on the other side. As Christians, we are baptised in water as a symbol of saying goodbye to one way of life and hello to a new life in Christ (Romans 6:3–4). Crossing over these boundaries involves saying goodbye to some familiar things and saying hello to what comes next. The water may be turbulent, there may even be rapids and we may not have a clue how deep it is, but we have to strike out and cross over, trusting in God's promises that we will not be overwhelmed and that we will not be on our own.

Saying goodbye in order to say hello

The Bible is full of stories about people who have had to say goodbye to things in order to be able to say hello to new things, to move on to new ways of life in response to God's call. God is always leading us on into new and fuller life. In Mark's gospel, the disciples are fishing as usual in the Sea of Galilee when Jesus comes by and calls them to follow him. They put down their nets, say goodbye to their familiar way of life and follow him into a new one (Mark 1:16–20).

We might find ourselves called to let go when all we want to do is to hold on and for things to stay the same forever. But the nature of life is change, and we have to let go if new things are to have room to grow.

Goodbye is not forever

When a loved one dies, it may seem as though we are separated from them by an immense sea and we cannot see where they have gone beyond the horizon. But when we do have to say goodbye, it is not forever, because the promise of Jesus is that eventually we will all be reunited; then we will see face to face and know what lies over that horizon (1 Thessalonians 4:17; 1 Corinthians 13:12–13). God has promised that there will be a glorious and unimaginable hello on the other side of whatever stormy waters we have to cross:

> A ship sails and I stand watching till she fades on the horizon and someone at my side says, 'She is gone.' Gone where? Gone from my sight, that is all. She is just as large now as when I last saw her. Her diminished size and total loss from my sight is in me, not in her. And just at the moment when someone at my side says, 'She is gone', there are others who are watching her coming over their horizon and other voices take up a glad shout: 'There she comes!' That is what dying is.[25]

In John's gospel, Peter and the disciples are fishing again on the Sea of Galilee after the death of Jesus. Jesus appears on the shore and, when John recognises him and tells Peter, Peter plunges straight into the water to meet his risen Lord. He saw the person he loved and longed to see again and waded in across the sea to get to him (John 21:1–14). How he must have longed to be with Jesus again and here he was, making breakfast for them: a glorious and unimaginable hello!

9

Sleeping tight

Blissful slumber

It's funny that we call the areas in the garden in which we plant seeds and bulbs 'beds'. Yet it makes sense, especially when we plant in the autumn as if expecting these embryonic plants to hibernate through the winter before waking in the new year. This planting is an act of faith; the dry papery bulbs or tiny brown seeds don't look very promising, yet we trust that come spring there will be vibrant green shoots pushing their way through the earth. And when this happens, we rejoice at a small miracle.

Something goes on under the ground that transforms what looked so unpromising into something both so different and so much better than could ever have been imagined. If you didn't know where daffodils came from, you'd laugh in disbelief at the pictures on the packets of bulbs.

We are finding the same thing with sleep. Sleep was always respected by ancient peoples, but in modern times scientists have not known what to make of it until quite recently. It seemed redundant. Why waste a third of our lives on it? Why not burn the candle at both ends?

But we are now beginning to understand that a good night's sleep is not an optional extra in life. All sorts of repairs and transformations of body and brain take place as we sleep. Rising from our beds, then, is perhaps not so different from the rising of the shoot from its bed of soil. We awake transformed. That's why 'sleeping on it' is a wise practice.

A Jesus kind of thing

We saw in chapter 7 that sharing bread with others was a Jesus kind of thing. But he was also fascinated by where the bread came from – the grain and its natural history. Just as breaking bread was a Jesus habit, the seed transformed to something different and unimaginably better was a Jesus obsession. It's the bass note of the kingdom.

Jesus plays with this image in all sorts of ways (see, for example, Mark 4:3–9, 26–29, 30–32; John 12:24). It's about unrecognised potential (the mustard seed is tiny and insignificant). It's about continuity even in the face of radical change (the mustard tree isn't anything like the seed, but it's a mustard tree not an apple tree). It's about sacrifice in the interests of something much better (the grain of wheat must die if the plant is to grow). It's about not being able to go back (you can't fit the plant back into the seed once it's germinated). It's about waiting around for ages when there are no signs that anything is actually happening. It's about important stuff that happens unobserved in the dark. It's about risk (not all the seed germinates and not all the shoots survive). It's about giving something back (the harvest gives food; the birds find a home in the tree). It's about mystery and transformation. It's about rising up – and so it's about resurrection.

It's also about Jesus himself. He is the seed who is placed in the ground and rises, and like the first snowdrop that pushes up through the soil, he is a pledge of more to come:

> But now is Christ risen from the dead, and become the firstfruits of them that slept.
>
> 1 CORINTHIANS 15:20 (KJV)

Notice how Paul brings resurrection, germination and waking from sleep together in this short sentence!

Jesus also talks about having to go down into the 'heart of the earth' for three days (Matthew 12:40). Have you ever wondered what was going on between the time Jesus' tomb was sealed and when he burst out of it on Easter morning? The answer is that nobody knows. Something amazing must have been happening in the dark when from outside it looked as if the story of Jesus was over, for he emerged from the tomb transformed. The New Testament tells us that when people met the risen Jesus, they didn't recognise him at first because, like the mustard tree, he was so different from the person they had known. But eventually they realised that he was different-but-the-same. What's more, he wasn't a ghost; he had a body with wounds, and he ate real food: fish and, of course, bread (Luke 24:37–48; John 20:27; 21:4–9).

Spiritual bodies not disembodied spirits

It follows, then, that when we die, we will be transformed into someone different-but-the-same as we are now. This is a bit vague, and it seems to have been a bit too vague for the first Christians in the church at Corinth because Paul felt the need to address this question with them:

> But someone will ask, 'How are the dead raised? With what kind of body do they come?'
> 1 CORINTHIANS 15:35

It's tremendously difficult to explain – in fact, as we have seen, Paul described it as a 'mystery' – so he sensibly reached for the Jesus image of the seed. He said that human beings are buried with bodies that perish, with all sorts of issues relating to shame or worthlessness, with human weaknesses and limitations, and with a perspective of this earth; but they will be raised with bodies that don't perish, in dignity and glory, fit and strong, and with a heavenly perspective (1 Corinthians 15:42–44). This won't happen immediately, but on the day that Jesus returns. Until then, the dead sleep, waiting to be called by the equivalent of an alarm clock – 'the last trumpet' (1 Corinthians 15:52).

There is no question of people's disembodied spirits floating around. The dead are not ghosts; they are sleeping. The New Testament as a whole paints a picture of the dead resting in the presence of God and able to worship him in their sleep, so they are not totally unconscious.

Even so, we often have a strong sense when someone dies that their spirit has been released from their physical body, especially if that body is frail or full of pain. Another image – this time not one found in the Bible – may be helpful here. This is the image of the butterfly, which begins life as an egg, hatches as a caterpillar, weaves a cocoon for itself and then finally emerges as a beautiful winged creature. Again, unless you knew where butterflies came from, you'd laugh in disbelief if someone showed you a chrysalis. When the winged creature emerges, it casts off the shell of the chrysalis. This is the remains of the butterfly's old body; it now has a wonderful new body, different-but-the-same as it had before. It's as if it has been released. But the winged creature isn't a disembodied spirit. It's just a radically different kind of body. We might think of death as the point at which the release from the chrysalis happens and resurrection as the point at which the butterfly takes to the air.

But these are all just pictures and they only give us glimpses of the mystery of the resurrection life.

Sleep tight

When someone dies, we instinctively feel that it is important to 'lay them to rest' properly. This doesn't just apply to our loved ones, though it's especially true for them; we feel that this is what every individual deserves.

When a person is dying, our wish is for their passing to be peaceful. By this, we may mean that there is little in the way of pain or discomfort for them, that they are surrounded by loved ones or that they have 'made their peace' where relationships had been broken. Another angle on departing in peace is given by Simeon, as he held the infant Jesus in his arms in the temple in Jerusalem (Luke 2:25–32). Simeon didn't feel he could leave this earth until he had seen this sign of hope for the future of the world. It wasn't all about him or all about the past. We sometimes see this in elderly people who seem to 'hang on' until a great-grandchild makes an appearance.

So, 'departing in peace' takes different forms for different people, but we all share the experience that to sleep properly we need some peace and quiet; that's the theme of Jill Murphy's wonderful book *Peace at Last*.[26] That's why part of saying goodbye to the deceased involves a sense of tucking them in for the night, or placing them in the arms of God. This is especially poignant when the deceased is a child. But it's also something that can be a healing experience where an adult's last illness has involved restlessness or insomnia.

Throwing earth into the grave, placing one's hand on the coffin as the 'commendation' is read, burying the person with a soft toy or a pillow – these can all be important aspects of this, as is the choice of restful music (even sometimes a lullaby) for the funeral service. And these gestures of setting somebody up for a long and refreshing sleep are readily understood by even quite young children.

One of the Church of England prayers of commendation sums this up well:

N has fallen asleep in the peace of Christ.
We entrust *him/her*, with faith and hope in everlasting life,
to the love and mercy of our Father
and surround *him/her* with our love and prayer.[27]

10

Being loved

In chapter 2, we listed some of the things that make death so troubling to us. Two of these – the fact that it is undergone alone and that it seems to wipe people out – turn out to be connected with each other in perhaps unexpected ways.

Alone again, naturally?

One of the most difficult things about death is that you can't subcontract it. That's why death is often described as the great leveller. Each of us undergoes our own death. Being completely alone is one of our deepest human fears, and we seem to have a horror of the idea of people dying alone.

Yet no matter how many people are around the deathbed, it's something the dying person has to do for his or herself. People who are dying perhaps know this instinctively; it's common for them to 'slip away' when relatives have popped out to go to the loo or to get a drink. You seem to need a bit of headspace in order to make the final move from life to death.

What's more, it's something that is a closed experience to those around the dying person. We can't reach out in solidarity in our usual way by saying things like, 'I remember when I had *my* first baby,' or, 'I hope your root canal work doesn't feel as agonising as *mine* did,' or, 'When I lost *my* mum…', all of which usually finish with 'but it got better in the end'. We just have to watch and pray.

Because of this, death is the ultimate mystery. Despite the numerous reports of near-death experiences, no one has ever come back from the dead and told us what it is like:

A Zen master asked by his student to tell him about death said he knew nothing about the topic. 'How can that be so?' said the student. 'A master must surely have knowledge of such things!' To which the master replied, 'Ah, but I am not a dead Zen master.'[28]

Follow me

But are we as alone as we think? Famous words from Psalm 23 say, 'Yea, though I walk through the valley of the shadow of death, I will fear no evil: for thou art with me' (Psalm 23:4, KJV). Unlike the Zen master, Jesus has gone through death before us and come back. He doesn't tell us exactly what it was like for him, but he does show us that death can be survived, and he invites us to follow him into it. The letter to the Hebrews describes him as a 'pioneer' (Hebrews 2:10; 12:2) – trailblazer – and 'forerunner' (Hebrews 6:20) – the person who goes ahead to reconnoitre. Jesus himself promised that he was going ahead to get a room ready for us (John 14:2). He didn't give details about the process of dying, but what he did say was that it would be okay as long as we stick with him; and he promised not to let us go (John 11:25; 6:39).

Yet this is not all about me and Jesus on our own private trip. It's easy to forget that the Bible talks about a whole host (literally) of companions who wish us well. Hebrews not only reminds us that Jesus has led the way through death but also that we are surrounded by a 'cloud of witnesses' (Hebrews 12:1) – heroes and heroines of the Old Testament who were faithful to God, many of whom suffered greatly, and who have gone before us and await our arrival to make them complete. The book of Revelation talks of saints and angels worshipping God around his heavenly throne. We remember this in our service of Holy Communion, when we say that we join with 'the whole company of heaven' to praise God here and now, singing, 'Holy, holy, holy.'

This may all sound a bit weird and far-fetched. Yet we shouldn't forget how comforting the idea of heavenly companions and angels can be to those who have lost loved ones, especially babies and young children, who are often said to have gone and joined them. Whatever we make of this picture language, the bottom line is this: you are not on your own.

You are special

You are not on your own in a cold, dark grave, and you do not travel the journey of death alone. This understanding of dying as being something that we do with both earthly and heavenly midwives is powerfully expressed in the eighth-century prayer known as the *Proficiscere*. This way of saying goodbye to the dying person is at the same time a reminder that she or he is part of something much bigger:

> Set out, Christian soul, from this world.
> In the name of God, the Father Almighty, who created you.
> In the name of Jesus Christ, Son of the living God, who suffered
>   for you.
> In the name of the Holy Spirit, who was poured out upon you.
> In the name of angels and archangels.
> In the name of thrones and dominations.
> In the name of principalities and powers and of all the heavenly
>   authorities.
> In the name of cherubim and seraphim.
> In the name of the human race, which is sustained by God.[29]

Note the way the first few lines of this prayer use the word 'you' to focus on the dying person's importance as an individual and then the focus broadens out. This is an odd but important paradox: each of us is special to God for our own sake, and yet part of our specialness is that we have a *place* in God's cosmic community.

It's telling that we describe jobs as 'posts', 'positions' or 'situations', and young people who get into university talk of being 'awarded a place'. Part of what is so good about the phone call with the job offer is that it gives you a *place* in life, and of course your sense of self-worth goes up as well. The two are connected.

We are not robots, but unique created beings who cannot be replicated, and we each have our unique place in God's sight and unique role in his kingdom.

Because we're worth it

> As for mortals, their days are like grass; they flourish like a flower of the field; for the wind passes over it, and it is gone, and its place knows it no more.
>
> PSALM 103:15–16

We don't like the idea of being wiped out by death. It is natural for us to want a trace of ourselves to remain – to have made our mark on this earth, to have built something worthwhile to pass on to our children. This also gives us a sense of security, self-worth and dignity. Yet we can get a bit too attached to the idea of finding our self-worth in our achievements and possessions. This seems to be a particular danger in our consumerist society, where people, especially young people, are increasingly defined by what they buy and the image they present on social media. Jesus told a story about a man who clung to his possessions in order to give himself a false sense of security. It finishes with these words:

But God said to him, 'You fool! This very night your life is being demanded of you. And the things you have prepared, whose will they be?'
LUKE 12:20

The man's attitude is the complete opposite of that of the flowers of the field:

They neither toil nor spin, yet I tell you, even Solomon in all his glory was not clothed like one of these.
MATTHEW 6:28–29

The psalmist had noticed that the flowers are short-lived. Jesus agreed, but he also noticed that they are beautiful and that, like the sparrows in the marketplace (Matthew 10:29–31), each one is unique and of special worth.

In her poem 'When death comes',[30] Mary Oliver writes of wanting to have made of her life 'something particular and real', yet instead of detailing what she is going to buy or build, she follows Jesus and says that she will think of each person's life as a flower 'as common as a field daisy, and as singular'.

We don't have to prove that we are better than the other flowers; we don't have to be ashamed of only being a common daisy, one among many; we don't have to try to make ourselves different or special. We have been *created* special, and God loves us for who we are. So, we can rejoice in our fellow daisies and, because perfect love casts out fear (1 John 4:18), we need not be afraid.

11

Finding safe spaces

Home sweet home

In the previous chapter, we saw how dignity and self-worth are closely connected with belonging – with having our unique place in something bigger. But 'our place' is also somewhere we can call home.

In the Bible, when Jesus tells his disciples that he is going to have to leave them, they are understandably upset. Jesus comforts them, telling them that he is going back to where his heavenly Father dwells, to prepare a place for them, so that one day they can be together again (John 14:2–3). Beyond everything else, we can be assured that there is a special place prepared for each one of us with God. This is a place where we are loved and accepted as we are, however we are feeling, just like in a loving home. In the story of the prodigal son (Luke 15:11–32), we see this 'welcome home' in action. The youngest son has gone off and spent all his inheritance, ending up in poverty. When he gets desperate, he decides to swallow his pride, return home and ask for forgiveness. His father sees him returning in the distance and, rather than condemning or accusing him, he meets him with compassion and welcomes him home with open arms, celebrating his return to the place where he belongs. There is a place waiting and ready to receive him, a place of acceptance, comfort and joy.

A safe haven and a secure base

If we have a happy home, it is the place we run to in times of trouble and the place from which we venture forth with confidence into the world. As we grow up, we carry this sense of home around with us in our heads, and it helps us to face life with strength. Sometimes, when life threatens to overwhelm us, we may actually say, 'I want to go home!'

This sense of inner security develops gradually over childhood as the child takes greater and greater steps of independence, marked by some significant milestones, such as the first day at 'big school'. Many younger children carry their 'home' around with them in the form of a particular soft toy or blanket. Research has shown that children look at large spaces differently from adults, quickly identifying the areas where it might be fun to explore and those where they can run to and hide. Church buildings can provide great opportunities for this. Children make maps of the world where some places are marked out as safe, working this out in games like 'off the ground tig'.

As we saw in chapter 5, if we are to face difficult realities, including talking about mortality, we need to feel reasonably safe, to be 'held' as we step into a place that may be dark or dangerous. One way that this can be communicated to children is by signalling safe spaces in the sessions by keeping boundaries clear (for example, by keeping to the convention that we don't talk directly to them about difficult stuff during the celebration at the end), and by supporting them in identifying safe places (games, rhymes, Bible verses, imagined lovely places, a corner of the building) that are there for them to run to and to venture out from. Remember that churches have a long and honourable history of providing 'sanctuary' (literally a place of safety) and that church buildings usually have a part called the 'sanctuary'. If your Seriously Messy service is in such a building, you may be able to explore this idea of sanctuary in the session or celebration.

Thin places

Of course, God is our ultimate safe place, our rock of ages to whom we can run in time of trouble and on whom we can build our lives. This special place with God is always there for us because God is always with us, however difficult things may be. It's just that sometimes we forget it, are too preoccupied to see it or are trying so hard to find God that we miss the fact that God is right here in the place we happen to be. In the Bible story of Jacob's dream, Jacob goes on a long journey and, when he is tired, sets up camp for the night. He lies down on the ground to get some sleep. It's an unpromising, dry and stony place, and there's only a stone to use for a pillow. But he has an amazing dream. He sees a ladder reaching from earth to heaven with angels going up and down it, and the Lord comes and stands beside him, promising to bless and keep him and to stay with him. Jacob awakes and realises that this unpromising place is a point at which heaven touches earth. God is present, though he did not know it before, 'This is none other than the house of God, and this is the gate of heaven' (Genesis 28:17). It turns out to be a special, holy place after all.

There are geographical locations or points in our life journey that can have this quality for us, where we become acutely aware that God is close. It's as if we get a glimpse of heaven in the here and now. Often these places can appear unpromising, for example, as we undergo a period of illness or spend time with a frail older person or an unruly child. Yet they turn out to be holy. It is good to look back over our lives and identify where this has been true for us and what we have learnt about heaven from such experiences. It's also good to revisit these places that have become a special part of our faith story.

Marking grief and making meaning

Although we have advised that people should not lead or participate in these sessions if they are freshly bereaved, many of us carry grief from long ago. We can never fully escape it. Sometimes it comes back and takes us by surprise.

When someone we love dies, we can feel a wide range of emotions, from initial shock and disbelief that this has happened to anger and deep sadness. Different feelings may come and go at different times, but it is well recognised that a process of grieving, however long it takes, is a natural human response to the experience of loss. This is often a messy time of stormy and painful emotions. At such times, we all need to find safe and supportive places where we can express our grief in our own way, so that in time, we can find healing for our lives and a special place within them for the person we love who has died. We are also likely to feel disorientated and lost, and we may feel the need for landmarks to help us negotiate what can be a confusing journey.

It may be helpful here to recall the story of Abraham, who, at an advanced age, set out into a strange land, but was able to make sense of it by building altars to mark his places of encounter with God (Genesis 12:7–8; 13:18), just as Jacob would later mark his 'thin place' with a sacred stone (Genesis 28:18, 22). One of the things that may well be going on in a good Seriously Messy session is a mental landmark-making, but it's played out in real physical space: isn't it interesting that traditionally the sanctuary of a church is where the altar is? The safe place is the sacred place, the place of meaning and encounter with God.

Each one of us is unique so we will each find our own place(s) for grief and ways of marking it; it may be a place of shared memories, a place within our own mind or in nature, or in the context of the loving support of other people. Grief takes many different forms and children have their own ways of grieving and making meaning.[31]

However, in our society, it can be difficult for people of any age to find those necessary places of understanding and acceptance because, as we have seen, our culture finds it hard to acknowledge death.

In the past, certain mourning rituals, such as wearing black for a time after a death, gave people permission to grieve and signalled to society that they needed space to do that. Secular society no longer has recognised social structures that support bereaved people in this way. The journalist Colin Brazier recently wrote an article following the death of his wife called 'Let funerals be sad', in which he said that he felt 'ill at ease' with the modern trend to wear bright clothes at funerals and to insist that they be only about 'rejoicing in a life now passed'.[32] Not to be allowed to be sad or to cry is too much to expect of the children, if not the adults, he says, and wearing black gives permission for people to be the way they feel. Having opportunities to express our grief and to have it accepted and validated by others is crucial to the healing process.

'Jesus wept'

The Bible is full of accounts of people mourning the death of loved ones; it is natural to lament, to weep and to cry out against the loss and tragedy of life. 'Jesus wept' (John 11:35) is one of the most human sentences in the Bible and speaks directly to our own experience. When Jesus met the friends and family of Lazarus, all weeping because Lazarus had died, Jesus himself was moved to tears. The psalms are also full of grief and lament. For example, in Psalm 31, the writer cries out for help: 'Be gracious to me, O Lord, for I am in distress; my eye wastes away from grief, my soul and body also' (Psalm 31:9). We can call out to God in our distress because God understands, loves and accepts us as we are in the sad as well as the happy times in life. In John's gospel, right at the beginning of the Christian story, we may recall Mary standing outside Jesus' tomb, weeping, grieving for her beloved friend and Lord (John 20:11).

God is always there for us, but because life can be messy and confusing, sometimes we don't recognise that. At such times, we need to create safe places for each other where we can come home to ourselves, be as we are and have space to find peace and to feel God close to us. Once we understand what people who are grieving might need, we can create safe places in our church where, if they wish, they can express their feelings or simply have someone alongside them as an expression of Christ's presence with them.

The sessions in this book offer different ways of exploring with all our senses what it is that we need to do to mark what we are going through, whatever age we are. They are places of gentle exploration that can hold people safely through the messiness of thinking about the prospect of death or recalling death from their past.

Part III

Session material

Session 1: Remembering

Messy reflection

> For I received from the Lord what I also passed on to you: the Lord Jesus, on the night he was betrayed, took bread, and when he had given thanks, he broke it and said, 'This is my body, which is for you; do this in remembrance of me.' In the same way, after supper he took the cup, saying, 'This cup is the new covenant in my blood; do this, whenever you drink it, in remembrance of me.'
>
> 1 CORINTHIANS 11:23–25 (NIV)

Jesus left his disciples ways to remember him, particularly the 'memory meal', which reminded them first of all of the Passover story, but now also of Jesus' death and resurrection. He said, 'Do this in remembrance of me.' It would perhaps have been more pleasant for the disciples not to have remembered Jesus' death, but Jesus actively wants them to remember it and to remember him. He knows what they need, and he knows what we need – both to remember him and to deal with the loss of other people we love. Remembering comes from the root of re-membering, of putting members or limbs back together again to make something whole. Sometimes remembering will make us sad, just as Jesus' friends must have been a little sad every time they remembered the happy times they had had with him. But sadness is fine, and we don't need to be scared of being sad. (Families may be aware of the 2015 Disney Pixar animated film about emotions, *Inside Out*, in which the character Sadness has a vital part to play.) Part of the value of remembering other people who have died (or are no longer with us for other reasons) is that this helps us know that when we ourselves are no longer there, people will remember us: our life is significant; we are loved; we matter to God and we matter to the people around us.

Today's theme is about remembering people we love who aren't near us anymore. Jesus' friends really missed him when he left them and they had a special way of remembering him. Today, we're remembering people we love in lots of different ways.

How does this session help people grow in Christ?

The session helps people understand that being human involves both joy and sorrow, love and loss. It is part of the gradual learning that Christ is there with us in all parts of life, not just the happy times.

Activities

1 Embossed photo frame

You will need: 8" x 6" rectangles of stiff, thick card (like corrugated cardboard from packing boxes); adhesive aluminium foil tape (try online – about £5 for 10m); cocktail sticks, pencils or playdough tools

Invite people to make a photo frame to take home and use to display a photo of someone they want to remember. Stick tape around the edges of the card, then press into the tape with a tool (pencil, cocktail stick or playdough tool) to make patterns in the tape.

Talk about your favourite memory of that person. I wonder whether Jesus' friends would have wanted a photo of him to keep after he had left them.

2 Plank plaques

You will need: thick twine or string; short pieces of wood; PVA glue in squirty bottles; pencils; drill (optional)

If you want to, drill a hole in either end of the plank so you can hang it up later. This could be done beforehand or as part of the activity. Ask people to think of one word that they associate with the person they want to remember who isn't with them anymore. Write this word in connected letters (joined-up writing) to fill the whole plank. Then squirt glue exactly over the writing. Carefully press the string down on to the word, following the glue line, so that the word is spelled out in string.

Talk about what word Jesus' friends might have thought of when they remembered Jesus. What word comes to mind when you think of Jesus?

3 Memory sticks

You will need: sticks with bark on from the garden, park or forest; potato peelers; paint; paint brushes

Younger people may simply make a pointy end and use it to draw in the earth or paint their stick in different colours as a reminder of something about the person they're remembering. Older people can whittle their stick safely with the peelers, creating either a pattern of stripes to represent both brighter and sadder memories of someone; or another pattern that represents that person in some way – for example, spots because they used to wear a spotty dress, crosses because they went to church or Xs because they gave you big kisses. Or simply make marks on the stick and think about the mark they made on your life. (People will come up with their own great ideas.)

Talk about how good it is to share memories of someone you love and tell stories about what they did

4 Forget-me-nots

> You will need: small flowerpots; things to decorate them
> (see suggestions below); forget-me-not seeds; compost
> (an alternative is rosemary cuttings, as these are free
> from someone with a rosemary bush and rosemary is the
> traditional plant for remembrance)

Decorate your flowerpots in one of the following ways or using an even better idea you've found online: self-adhesive mosaic squares; turn them upside down and dribble acrylic paint over them in interesting patterns; choose a cartoon character your person particularly liked and paint your flowerpot as a stylised version of that character; grout the pot and stick pebbles or shells on; paint them first with blackboard paint and allow to dry, then provide liquid chalk pens or chalk to decorate with.

Fill the pots with compost and either plant the seeds or provide seeds in a sachet to take home if it's not the right season.

Talk about the way we can remember someone through our senses. When we see them or smell these plants or flowers, they may remind us of the person we love. Jesus gave his friends food and drink to remember him by taste. What senses do you use when you remember someone you love?

5 Poor person's Kintsukuroi

> You will need: unwanted ceramic plate, bowl or mug;
> superglue; plastic bag; PVA glue; glitter (or glitter glue);
> pictures of Kintsukuroi

You might want to do just one stage of this activity as each one is quite time-consuming. It also involves sharp edges and superglue at various stages, so take the necessary precautions, depending on whom you're involving.

Put your ceramic object in a plastic bag, make sure the opening is closed, and drop it on to a hard surface – you want it to be broken but not smashed into smithereens, so try dropping it from knee height.

Fit the pieces back together like a jigsaw. (Mind the sharp edges, of course). Superglue them in place.

Mix the PVA glue with a lot of glitter and use to spread over and into the cracks. Allow to dry.

Speedier versions of this have been suggested on Facebook, such as broken biscuits glued with icing. (Thank you, Kathy Bland!)

Talk about the feelings of brokenness you have when you lose somebody. We will never be the same as we were before we lost that person, but we can still be put back together again as something beautiful. These plates aren't incredibly beautiful, because we're not skilled craftspeople, but Japanese craftspeople can make gorgeous works of art from brokenness called Kintsukuroi. God is an even greater craftsperson than they are, and our lives are in God's hands.

6 Marbling chocolate

You will need: different-coloured Fairtrade chocolate bars (milk, plain, dark); small bowls; means of melting, e.g. microwave or bowls of hot water (used under supervision); stirrers or skewers; baking paper; cocktail stick or lolly sticks; spoons; sheets of suitable shapes, such as circles, diamonds, triangles

Melt small amounts of chocolate in small bowls. Place the shape templates underneath the baking paper so the shape shows through. Use the spoon to dribble melted chocolate of one colour into the shape. It will go over the edges but that's fine. Dribble a smaller amount of a different coloured chocolate over the top of the first chocolate. Use a skewer to gently marble the two colours together.

Try not to lose their distinctiveness. Put a cocktail stick or lolly stick into the shape to serve as a handle once it has set.

Talk about the way the colours mix together to make something beautiful. Some times in life are both sad and happy at the same time, and it's okay for our emotions to be mixed together. We don't need to feel bad about that. It might even be something beautiful.

7 Thoughtful toast

> **You will need: toaster; sliced bread; food colouring; brushes; heart-shaped cutter; butter or spread; butter knives**

Invite people to paint one piece of bread in one colour or pattern and another piece in a different colour or pattern, or to work in pairs and paint one each. Toast them (the colours will show up much more brightly after toasting). Cut a heart shape out of each piece of toast and fit the heart back into the 'wrong' piece of bread. Spread it with butter and eat it.

Talk about how different the toast looks with the different-coloured heart in it. When we love someone, we find a place in their heart (like the heart-shaped hole in the toast) and they find a place in ours and neither of us will be the same person afterwards, even when we're no longer in the same place. Talk about the way Jesus gave his friends a meal to remember him by.

8 Candles

> **You will need: tin foil; night lights; matches; ways to extinguish fire**

Decide on a 'safe area' and cover the floor with tin foil. Invite people to light a candle in memory of somebody they aren't with any more for whatever reason and to place it on the foil. (This was done at Portsmouth Cathedral during the Moonlight Walk for cancer and made a very moving spectacle, as more and more nightlights reflected back from the foil.)

Talk about any feelings that people want to talk about, or just leave space to be silent together.

9 Memory foam

> **You will need: washing-up liquid; water; food colouring; blender; squeezy bottles; chalk; a pavement**

Mix a few drops of washing-up liquid, a mug of water and a few drops of food colouring in a blender. Pour the mixture into a squeezy bottle. Have different colours for different parts of the pavement: blue for sad memories; yellow for happy memories; red for angry memories; green for thankful memories. Invite people to draw patterns on that part of the pavement and to recall sad, happy, angry and thankful memories about somebody they are no longer near, while they 'doodle'. Have some chalk nearby in case people want to draw with those instead.

Talk about the way that nobody except Jesus is perfect and all of us have a mixture of memories about people we've loved. We can ask God to help us be thankful or to forgive.

10 Big-hearted knot challenge

> **You will need: paracord; a long piece of rope; a picture of a simple heart-shaped Celtic knot**

Try this in two stages. Using the picture as a guide, first tie a heart-shaped knot with the paracord at the table, then tie it in an enormous way on the floor with as long a piece of rope as you can manage – the bigger the better, as it will feel more 'rugged'. If you want a tamer version of this activity, you could simply print off a knot picture and colour it in.

Talk about the way we go on loving people even when they're no longer there. And while this rope has a beginning and an end, God's love for us goes on and on and has no beginning and no end, rather like the knot itself in the picture.

Celebration

And God remembered

What are human beings that you are mindful of them, mortals that you care for them?
PSALM 8:4

Invite stories and comments on the different activities. Bring out the theme of remembering and how important our memory is.

Ask everyone for examples of their earliest memory. Ask everyone for examples of their happiest memory. Ask family groups for examples of special shared memories.

Memory is one of the important gifts that God has given us. God made us like God, and memory is part of the nature of God.

With this gift, we can remember places, special events in our life, important moments and of course people, even when they're no longer with us.

But our memories aren't perfect.

There is an old story about that, from the Hebrew Midrash tradition and in particular the story of creation:

Back at the beginning of time, just before God created people, God consulted with the angels as to what gifts he ought to give them. All sorts of ideas were put forward: love, joy, hope, strength, good looks, intelligence and laughter. Then God suggested, 'What about the gift of remembering or the gift of forgetting?'

The singing angels said that, yes, people should have the gift of remembering, so that they could sing heavenly songs, but they shouldn't have the gift of forgetting, because then they wouldn't remember the music and so couldn't go on singing!

The story angels said that, yes, people should have the gift of remembering but not of forgetting, because then they wouldn't remember what happened next and so couldn't tell stories properly!

The naming angels said that, yes, people should have the gift of remembering but not of forgetting, because then they wouldn't remember what they were naming and so could become confused as to what they had named and what they hadn't!

God smiled and then asked one angel about what she remembered. Immediately, the angel began telling God that she remembered how once another angel had stepped on her robe and tore it, and the tear was still there!

Another angel remembered how once some of the other angels had borrowed his halo to play frisbee and that they had ended up denting it!

And yet another angel remembered how some of the other angels had laughed at her first attempts to fly and how that still upset her!

One by one they all remembered things that carried hurts and recalled bad feelings and soon there was pandemonium in heaven.

When God saw that they remembered so much, God sighed and declared, 'Oh, just forget it!'

And so because of this, God decided to give people the gift of remembering *and* of forgetting.

It's because we forget (and yes, that too can be a gift) that we need things to help us remember. I wonder what good ideas you have for remembering something. It could be remembering things for a test or exam; it could be remembering birthdays; or it could be remembering important information that you have been asked to pass on to others.

Here are some ideas that may be mentioned: photos, special objects, Post-it notes, knots in handkerchiefs, reminders on our phones, diaries, little rhymes or word associations... or maybe visualising a special place or object.

All these things can help us a lot. In the same way, memory prompts are important to us when people die. We have a special service, often with special flowers and kind words full of memories. And we arrange a special 'memory place' for the body or the ashes. Perhaps we set up a special plaque, put some writing on a bench or headstone, or plant a rose. In times gone by, rich people even had statues made!

God wants us to remember and to be thankful for all the good memories we have shared with those who are no longer with us. These many memories help us to bring the person back again to our mind's eye. They are like pieces of a jigsaw that together recreate a picture of the person whom we loved and want to remember.

When Jesus was about to die, he gave his friends a way to remember him. It was a special meal with bread and wine.

Depending on your tradition, show the cup and the plate (chalice and paten) which your church uses for Communion.

Whenever Christians eat the bread and drink the wine, they remember Jesus – how he lived and died and how much he loves them and they love him.

Sometimes in a cemetery, a graveyard or another special place, we have words written to help us remember the people we love, such as 'You are always in our thoughts' or 'Remember me'. At some graves, you can also find photos, pictures or objects associated with the person's life. All these things help us not to forget. But even so, it isn't always easy to remember and to keep memories alive.

But be encouraged: God is the one who gave us the gift of memory, and God will help us remember the good things. He is the great Rememberer. Even when we forget, God never forgets. God helps us and because God remembers those people we love, they are alive with him forever.

Two very special words that come often in the Bible are these: 'God remembered.' Let's use these words as we hear about some very famous people in the Bible. (*Invite everyone to join in with the words in bold each time.*)

When there was no land in sight for poor Noah on the ark, and there seemed no hope,
God remembered Noah.

When Abraham was worried for his nephew caught up in a city that was about to be destroyed, and there seemed no hope,
God remembered Abraham.

When all was tears and despair for poor Hannah who couldn't have children, and there seemed no hope,
God remembered Hannah.

When David wrote sad songs of despair, and there seemed no hope,
God remembered David.

When, again and again in the Bible, the people were defeated, crushed and alone, and there seemed no hope,
God remembered those he loved.

And when we are sad because someone we love has died, and there seems no hope,
God remembers and will help us to remember too.

God always remembers his promises and his mercy, and God puts people back together again for us – God remembers them.

At the saddest and darkest time of Easter, Jesus talked about remembering. There was a thief who was being crucified next to Jesus, who said, 'Jesus remember me.' Jesus replied, 'Today you will be with me in heaven.' And Christians believe that promise is also for us and for those we love. Jesus always remembers us to God.

Even though our memories fail or fade – even if we forget – God's memory will never let us down in life or in death. Whether we live or whether we die, we will be safe, because God does not forget us.

Prayer

Invite everyone to go and collect one thing that they have made today that is particularly special and that will help them to remember those they love and to remember that God never forgets any of us.

Holding on to those objects and, after a short space for people to name individuals quietly before God, join together with these words, inviting them repeat the short phrases:

Thank you, remembering God,
for the gift of memory
and for your promise
that you will always remember us and those we love.

Song suggestions

'Remember me' – Friends and Heroes
'Jesus, remember me' – Taizé

Scripture references: Genesis 8 and 19; 1 Samuel 1; Psalm 132;
Luke 27.

Session 2:
Saying goodbye and hello

Messy reflection

Afterwards Jesus appeared again to his disciples, by the Sea of Galilee. It happened this way: Simon Peter, Thomas (also known as Didymus), Nathanael from Cana in Galilee, the sons of Zebedee, and two other disciples were together. 'I'm going out to fish,' Simon Peter told them, and they said, 'We'll go with you.' So they went out and got into the boat, but that night they caught nothing.

Early in the morning, Jesus stood on the shore, but the disciples did not realise that it was Jesus.

He called out to them, 'Friends, haven't you any fish?'

'No,' they answered.

He said, 'Throw your net on the right side of the boat and you will find some.' When they did, they were unable to haul the net in because of the large number of fish.

Then the disciple whom Jesus loved said to Peter, 'It is the Lord!' As soon as Simon Peter heard him say, 'It is the Lord,' he wrapped his outer garment round him (for he had taken it off) and jumped into the water. The other disciples followed in the boat, towing the net full of fish, for they were not far from shore, about a hundred metres. When they landed, they saw a fire of burning coals there with fish on it, and some bread.

Jesus said to them, 'Bring some of the fish you have just caught.' So Simon Peter climbed back into the boat and dragged the net ashore. It was full of large fish, 153, but even with so many the net was not torn. Jesus said to them, 'Come and have breakfast.' None of the disciples dared ask him, 'Who are you?' They knew it was the Lord. Jesus came, took the bread and gave it to them, and did the same with the fish. This was now the third time Jesus appeared to his disciples after he was raised from the dead.

JOHN 21:1–14 (NIV)

Have you ever thought how many of the 'hello and goodbye' stories in the Bible happen near water? Water is something that separates one person from another, like the lake water separating Peter from Jesus in the story above, the Red Sea separating God's people from the Egyptians or the River Jordan separating them from the promised land. Water in baptism is a sign of this 'passing from one side to another', of going across some sort of frontier or boundary, entering new territory. It involves saying goodbye to some things and saying hello to others. When death divides us – like a great impassable sea – from the people we love, we feel the pain of separation; we cannot see across the barrier between us. But the promise of Jesus is that we will be reunited eventually; we will see face-to-face. The impetuous action of Peter in jumping into the water as soon as he recognises Jesus is an action that demonstrates that deep longing to be reunited with someone we love and have lost.

How does this session help people grow in Christ?

This session explores what it means to tolerate separation and to come to terms with it. It is not about denying its pain, but recognising it as part of the natural process of life and death, hello and goodbye.

Activities

1 Power boats

You will need: sponges; short lengths of plastic tubing about 2 cm diameter; balloons about 8 cm long; scissors (craft knives are easier but need more supervision); a paddling pool or baby bath filled with water

Cut one narrow end of the sponge into a point to make the prow of the boat. Cut a vertical slit from top to bottom in the centre of the sponge. Feed the balloon through the slit, blow it up, hold the air in by pinching the neck and fit the pipe into the neck of the balloon. Carefully lower the boat into the water with the tube pointing out backwards and see if it will cross from one side of the pool to the other when you release the air.

(Alternatively, provide a range of junk alongside the balloons and invite people to design their own boat to cross from one side to the other.)

Talk about journeys across the sea people have made. Ask about the goodbyes and hellos involved in those journeys.

2 Bridge-building

You will need: real water in a tub or a blue cloth to represent water; dried peas that have been soaked; cocktail sticks (or any bridge-building materials you have in stock); toy car

Challenge people to build a bridge using the materials available that will bear the weight of a toy car when it's pushed from one side to the other.

Talk about a local bridge and the way people on one side are separated from the people on the other. When someone we love dies, it can feel as if they have crossed over a bridge that we can't cross yet. It hurts, but Jesus promises that one day we will all be together again.

3 Mosaics

You will need: plenty of paint colour charts from DIY stores; scissors; backing paper or card; glue

Invite people to cut out squares of colour from the sample leaflets and glue them together in a mosaic design that goes from dark on one side to light on the other. It doesn't have to be a line – it could be any shape they like. It might be different shades of just one colour or it could be lots of colours together.

Talk about how it feels when we lose someone we love: when they die or move on or move away from us. It can feel very dark, especially at first. Saying goodbye is very hard. It might take a long time until things feel bright again and that's okay: we all need to say goodbye and say hello in our own time. Peter had to say goodbye to Jesus, his best friend, when Jesus died. In today's story, Peter gets the chance to say hello to Jesus again.

4 Water pistol art

You will need: water pistols; runny paint (half paint, half water); large sheets of paper attached to a wall (probably outside); masking tape (optional); protective clothing; a leader who is good at keeping control...

Have a water pistol for each colour of paint. Squirt the paper and enjoy the colours running together. You can put shapes on in masking tape and wait until the paint dries before you peel it off, or you can just fire away for fun. This activity may just have to finish in a water fight, so you may want to keep a couple of water pistols with clean water in them for this inevitable purpose.

Talk about people who got wet in Bible stories. What were they saying goodbye or hello to when they got wet? Why do you think baptism needs water? What are we saying goodbye and hello to when we are baptised?

5   Obstacle course

You will need: a corridor or room you can use just for this activity; strips of paper; sticky tape

Tape the strips of paper across the corridor in a random pattern, some high, some low, some diagonally. Invite people to get from one end of the course to the other without touching any paper. Adjust as you go on to make it easier or harder.

Talk about the way the obstacle course separates people at one end from the people at the other. In a little while, they will be able to be back together again, but for now they're divided. Jesus wants us to know that although we may be divided from people we love when they die, it won't be forever: we will get to say hello to them again when the time is right. It's very hard to be separated from them, but it won't be forever.

6   Waving hand

You will need: small pitta pouches cut in half; cream cheese or hummus; variety of fruit and vegetable sticks: celery, pepper, cucumber, apple, carrot, watermelon, etc.

Put some filling into the pitta pouch to act as glue, then imagine the pouch as the palm of a hand, and add four fingers and a thumb made from assorted fruit and vegetables stuck into the filling. Before you eat it, talk about waving hands…

(You could do this activity with a circular biscuit, icing as glue and chocolate fingers as fingers, but it's a tad less healthy.)

Talk about waving hands: does a wave mean goodbye or hello? It can mean both! There are times in life which are 'goodbye' times and other times which are 'hello' times. Christians know that when we wave goodbye to someone, perhaps when they die or when they move away, it is sad but it won't be goodbye forever: we know we will meet them again because that's what Jesus promises us.

7 Foil maze

You will need: tin foil; lids from shoeboxes or similar; marbles

Draw a stick-person on the inside edge of the box lid at one of the narrow ends. Write 'START' on the inside of the lid at the opposite end. Invite people to shape foil into the walls of a maze between the start and the stick-person so that they can challenge someone to roll a marble from the start to the stick-person. The aim is to reunite the stick-person with their marble by tilting the lid to send the marble through the maze without it falling out of the lid.

Talk about being reunited with people we love and whom we've lost, like the stick-person is separated from their marble but then reunited. When someone dies, we are separated from them and it can be really sad while we are apart. But Jesus brings all things together in the end: we will be together again one day.

8 DIY plumbing

You will need: plenty of plastic junk, especially bottles; lengths of tubing or pipes such as hosepipe; duct tape; tin foil; drawing pins; large base positioned upright against a wall; buckets; jugs; water

Invite people to create a watercourse that will channel water poured into the top container down to a bucket at the bottom, losing as little as possible on the way. Think Heath Robinson or Wallace and Gromit-type inventions.

Talk about water and how it divides lands from each other. What divides us from people we love who have died or moved away? What do Christians believe about meeting them again, and why do we believe that?

9 Quilling waves

> **You will need: quilling tools; quilling strips; glue; scissors; paper; examples from the internet**

There are some beautiful examples of this activity under a search for 'quilled wave' on the web – print off a few or have them available on a laptop for people to be inspired by. Invite them to have fun with this gentle craft of paper twirling to make their own quilled wave picture.

Talk about the verse from Song of Songs: 'Love is as strong as death... Many waters cannot quench love; rivers cannot sweep it away' (8:6–7, NIV). What does this say to you about love and death?

10 'Hi, bye!' hands

> **You will need: funky foam; pea sticks or pool noodles; sticky tape; felt-tip pens; list of words as below; face paints (if using alternate version below)**

Language	Hi	Bye
Mandarin	Ni hao	Zaijian
Croatian	Pozdravite	Pozdravite
Italian	Ciao	Ciao
Maori	Kia ora	Haere ra
French	Bonjour	Au revoir
German	Guten Tag	Auf Wiedersehen

Japanese	Kon'nichiwa	Sayonara
Dutch	Hallo	Tot ziens
Spanish	Buenos dias	Adios
Hindi	Hailo	Alavida

Draw round your hand on to the foam and cut it out. Pick the pair of 'Hi, bye' words from the table and write a 'hi' on one side of your hand and a 'bye' on the other. Tape the hand on to a pea stick or pool noodle and challenge people to be the fastest to hold up their 'hand' with the right side facing the front when you call out 'hi' or 'bye'. (Alternatively, you could write a 'hi' on one palm of your real hand and a 'bye' on the other, using face paint.)

Talk about the fact that both the 'hi' and the 'bye' are waves. In some languages, it's the same word for hi and bye! Have you had to say 'bye' to someone recently? How did that feel? Will it be forever?

Celebration

Waving hello, waving goodbye

> I am the First and the Last, the Living One who died, who is now alive forevermore.
> REVELATION 1:18 (TLB)

Invite feedback on the different activities in this session. What did they enjoy? Which activity meant most to them?

I wonder if you've ever watched an ocean liner leaving from a port or a yacht setting out to sea. If you had friends or family on board, you may have waved goodbye as the boat slowly disappeared out of sight. Or maybe you've experienced something similar when you've watched a train leave a railway station, a plane take off or a car set off on a journey. Those left behind wave goodbye, but someone else – at another port or station, in another country or in someone else's home – will soon be waving hello.

In this way, link waving to the themes of leaving and arriving, losing and gaining and particularly how saying goodbye means that someone, somewhere else is saying hello.

Waving is something all of us do from time to time. 'Wave goodbye… to Granny [Lindsey, or Mum]', we say to our children. Or, 'Give Grandpa [Olly, or Dad] a welcome wave', we may also say.

Invite everyone to wave in different ways: one-handed, with both hands, discreetly, enthusiastically, sadly or excitedly. Maybe you could also introduce a few silly 'waves' such as: a microwave (a very small wave), a tidal wave (a very large wave) and a radio wave (a wave accompanied by sound).

In fact, waving is one of the early examples of sign language that we learn as children. Coming and going, leaving and arriving, appearing and disappearing are part of life – something we learn very early on in our childhood. We even turn it into a game that children in particular can find very funny – the game of peekaboo.

Play this game, hiding and then appearing from behind something – including your own hands! This usually gets everyone laughing.

Though this is fun, it has a serious side to it. It teaches us to trust that someone is there even when we can't see them.

When Jesus died, his disciples thought that this was the final wave goodbye to their best friend. When the garden tomb was sealed with a stone, they thought it was goodbye forever. Then came the miracle and the excitement of Easter Day. Jesus was back from the dead, waving hello again to his friends. But Jesus was different. He wasn't easily recognised at first by many, and he didn't stay long in the same place. He kept coming and going. He waved hello and goodbye and then hello again many times. It was like a game of peekaboo for the 40 days after Easter. But it had a serious side too. Jesus was teaching them to trust him even though they couldn't always see him and soon wouldn't see him anymore. But he would always be with them.

Christians believe that Jesus' resurrection has turned all sad goodbyes into hopeful hellos. Even though we can't see those we love after they die, it is not a final goodbye. It may be goodbye from our point of view, but there is a big hello for them in heaven, like the ship going over the horizon.

In the Bible story today, Jesus was waving hello again to Peter, John and the others in the boat on Galilee. He could wave hello, because God had turned the sad goodbye of the cross into the great hello of the resurrection. But Peter, John and the others in the boat had to say goodbye again to Jesus because he had to return to heaven, where one day all goodbyes will become hellos forever – and there will be no more goodbyes.

'Hello' is among the first words that many of us learn and it has links to the words for health and wholeness. When Jesus says hello to us, Jesus is offering his health – his salvation – to us all.

'Goodbye' is an old English word that is a contraction of the phrase 'God be with you'. It is a prayer. Jesus' goodbye is a promise that God will be with us and those we love until we all meet again.

Prayer

Let's use waving hello and goodbye as part of our time of prayer together:

> We wave hello (*encourage everyone to wave hello*) to those we meet, wishing them good health and the very best in life.

We wave goodbye (*encourage everyone to wave goodbye*) to those who leave, wishing them God-speed and God's presence on their journey.

We wave hello (*encourage everyone to wave hello*) to each new life that is born, wishing them the best of health and happiness.

We wave goodbye (*encourage everyone to wave goodbye*) to those who die, trusting that God will be with them.

We wave goodbye (*encourage everyone to wave goodbye again*), but at the same time God waves hello (*encourage everyone to wave hello again*), welcoming them into heaven.

One day we will wave hello again (*encourage everyone to wave hello*) to those we love, because they have found their own hello in heaven.

God can turn all our goodbyes into hellos, because of God's great love for us.

Song suggestions

'Hello' – Fischy Music (From *We're On This Road*)
'Goodbye' – Fischy Music (From *We're On This Road*)
'Hello, Goodbye' – The Beatles

Session 3:
Sleeping tight

Messy reflection

> Very truly I tell you, unless a grain of wheat falls to the ground and dies, it remains only a single seed. But if it dies, it produces many seeds.
>
> JOHN 12:24 (NIV)

A buried seed looks dead but, when the time is right, it's transformed into a new plant. The plant looks nothing like the seed. A caterpillar inside a chrysalis looks as if it has no life, but again, at the right time, after being hidden away, it breaks out as a transformed butterfly. When we sleep, it looks as if nothing is going on, but in fact our brains and bodies are doing phenomenal amounts of work, restoring, filing, healing, so that we can wake up feeling like a new person: we are being transformed, even as we sleep!

Being human means being part of a cycle of life and death. Our bodies wear out and need to be buried or disposed of. Although this is in one way the end of us, Christians believe that there is a transformation at work and a new beginning waiting to happen. Just as the plant looks nothing like the seed but is recognisable as coming from it – just as we look at the butterfly and can hardly believe it was once that earthbound caterpillar – so, when the time is right, we will rise transformed and with a new heavenly body. What an exciting prospect!

We have no idea what we will look like. It doesn't really matter – we have all the information we need for living our lives well in our earthly bodies for now. It's a great mystery but also a deep comfort that even as we bury or cremate someone's body with love and care, we can be sure that the person's life goes on in a new and wonderful form. They don't become a disembodied spirit but instead will have a transformed body – just what they need for their new life in a new dimension.

Jesus must have been very conscious that he himself was soon to die, to be shrouded like a caterpillar in a chrysalis, and would then break out of the wrappings and the tomb and be raised to new life. His resurrection body would be different but recognisable to those who knew and loved him.

How does this session help people grow in Christ?

The session will help people to better understand Jesus' death and resurrection and to see how this pattern of death leading to transformed life takes place in our lives too.

Activities

1 Special words quiz

You will need: the quiz questions below displayed in some way that makes it easy to do the quiz together as a family

The idea of this quiz is to provide a starting point for conversations about the ways we deal with a body after someone has died. Children may know more about ancient Egyptian embalming than what happens in their own culture.

What is a crematorium?
a   A place where you make cream

b A place where you grow cremberries
c A place where you take bodies to be burned with respect
d A place where chickens lay creme eggs

What is a cemetery?
a Something a bit like a cement mixer
b A place where bodies are carefully placed in graves; a graveyard
c Half a Terry
d About the same as a centimetre

What is a coffin?
a A box specially made to put a body in
b A box to cough into
c A box to put your coffee in
d A toffee tin for your cough sweets

What is a funeral?
a A crowd of people saying, 'Phew!'
b A few people saying, 'Phew!'
c A more funnelly funnel
d A special service to say goodbye to someone who's died

What does 'bury' mean?
a A little round fruit
b To be very busy
c To be very furry
d To put something underground

Talk about the stories you might have around some of these concepts. They are deliberately very basic ones to allow people to take the conversation in the direction they want to go, based on their own experiences. The quiz will probably raise other questions or memories too, so you might like to invite someone like your minister or a local funeral director to be on hand to answer questions and talk sensitively about the local situation.

2 Transformation

> You will need: a selection of junk materials; sticky tape; pens; scissors; glue and other basic equipment
>
> OR clear used plastic bottles; butterfly shapes; fine marker pens; scissors; glue; mini magnets; nail varnish or glass paints

This activity is about transforming something that is no longer needed into something new and wonderfully different, rather like a caterpillar is transformed into a butterfly. You might either explain the concept of upcycling and transformation, then invite people to transform some junk into something new according to their own creativity.

Or create a butterfly fridge magnet. Cut a piece of plastic from a bottle, big enough to tape your butterfly shape on. Turn over the plastic and trace the outline of the butterfly shape and any details you want, using a marker pen. Remove the taped-on picture. Cut out the shape. Use the nail varnish or glass paints to colour in the shape. Allow to dry and stick the magnet on the reverse side. (Idea from Upcycling with The Body Shop Pinterest page, where you will find many other ideas for plastic bottles.)

Talk about the way things wear out and need to be laid to rest. But we are so precious to God that, even when it looks as if nothing is happening, he transforms the bodies we use on earth into new amazing bodies after we die. We don't know what they will be like, but we know they will be awesome!

3 Paper or plane

> You will need: paper; paper plane instructions from the internet

Make and fly paper planes.

Talk about the way that a flat sheet of paper, which does not move far if you try to flick it or shove it along, is transformed into something that flies and loops through the air – in a different dimension. It is the same sheet of paper but totally transformed. Our bodies are made to function in an earthly dimension, and, after we die, we will need to be transformed to function in a heavenly dimension.

4   Time for bed

> You will need: small pieces of felt; needles; thread; scissors; printed bedtime prayers, in a very small font size (optional)

Make a tiny sleeping bag out of a folded piece of felt, about 5 cm long. You might want to learn blanket stitch. Cut out a tiny felt person to tuck into it, along with a tiny copy of a bedtime prayer of your choice.

Talk about the way we carefully tuck each other up to go to sleep at night and the way we wake up the next morning full of energy and life and ready for the new day. It looks as though nothing is happening while someone is asleep, but in reality, they're being completely refreshed. You might want to ask if anyone has ever tucked in an animal that has died and laid it to rest (either a pet or a wild bird or animal they have found), what materials they used and how they did it. Enjoy wondering together about how they might be transformed within Jesus' love.

5   Leafing things behind

> You will need: a selection of dead leaves; metallic paint; fine paintbrushes; other colours of paint or good-quality coloured pens; glitter (optional)

Invite people to choose a dead leaf and to have a good look at it. Then transform the leaf to have a very different appearance by painting it or drawing and colouring on it. You might trace the veins in a different colour or paint a scene or something suggested by its shape. Add glitter if you want to get really messy!

Talk about the promise in the Bible that when the right moment comes, 'we will be changed' (1 Corinthians 15:52, NIV). We will need heavenly bodies for a heavenly experience. We're only changing the surface of these leaves, but our new bodies will be a complete change from our old ones. Which bits would you be happy to leave behind? Nothing you love will disappear: everything good will be there in some way. What a treat!

6 Baking

You will need: a simple baking recipe, such as one for cupcakes, sugar biscuits or cheese straws; the ingredients and equipment necessary

Bake together.

Talk about the way you have transformed the separate ingredients into something that looks, smells and tastes completely different – something that is now wonderful (though some will argue that the raw ingredients are equally wonderful). We don't know what our bodies will change into after we die, but we do know they will be different and wonderful.

7 Flapping butterfly experiment

You will need: balloons; tissue paper; scissors; template of a simple butterfly; pencils; drawing pins; a cork or a cork board

Use the stencil to cut out a simple butterfly shape from tissue paper. Pin the centre of it to the cork or board so that its wings lie flat to either side.

Rub the balloon on your hair and see if you can make the butterfly flap its wings by holding the balloon near the wings.

(Science: When you rub the balloon on your hair, the friction pulls small particles called electrons from the atoms of the balloon material. Electrons have a negative charge and give the surface of the balloon a negative charge. When you wave the balloon over the butterflies, the balloon pushes away the negatively charged electrons in the tissue paper and pulls positively charged particles (protons) towards it, making the tissue paper move.)

Talk about the life cycle of a butterfly and the way a crawling, earthbound caterpillar transforms into a flying butterfly. Talk about the way it looks as if nothing is happening when it's in the chrysalis, but in reality huge changes are taking place out of sight. We will be able to do such awesome things when we get our new bodies!

8   Now you seed it...

> **You will need: as many seeds, pips, stones and kernels as you can collect (from fruit you've eaten, your garden, a walk in the park or indeed your out-of-date seed packets); a photograph of what plant, tree or flower that seed would turn into if you planted it; an ice-cube tray**

Put the seeds into separate compartments of an ice-cube tray and display the photos around it. Invite people to match up the seed and the potential plant.

If you have spare seeds, give everyone a 'mystery selection' to take away and plant to see what grows.

Talk about Jesus' words in John 12:24: 'Very truly I tell you, unless a grain of wheat falls to the ground and dies, it remains only a single seed. But if it dies, it produces many seeds.' Jesus was putting words to the mystery of death. What stands out for you from his words?

9 Seed bombs

You will need: tissue paper or shredded paper (great use for recycling paper); packets of easy-to-grow garden seeds; water; food mixer

Soak the paper in some water for two minutes, then put it in the food mixer and blitz it until it's a pulp. Mould it in your hands and add a few pinches of seeds as you mush it together into a small ball shape. Allow to dry, and plant it at home by throwing it into the spot where you want it to sprout. (The seeds get wet from the wet paper, so advise people to plant them sooner rather than later or they may sprout in your take-home bag.)

Talk about what the seeds look like and what the pictures of the flowers on the seed packet look like. How amazing it is that they can be so different! In the same sort of way, we have no idea what we will be like in the age to come, but we know it will be amazing!

10 Chromato-butterflies

You will need: white coffee filter papers; thick soluble marker pens; water in cups; craft wire or pipe cleaners; invisible thread; coat hanger

Draw a circle quite heavily around the centre of your coffee filter paper, about 5 cm in diameter in one colour. Scrunch the coffee filter together so that the centre point forms the base point (like a flower) and place the centre point – NOT the colour circle – in the water. Watch as the water is drawn into the filter paper and the colour separates and flows. When the colour reaches the edge of the paper, remove it and spread it out to dry. Then pinch the paper together at the centre and fasten it with the wire or pipe cleaner, with the sides crumpled and spread like butterfly wings. Turn the ends of the wire into antennae and, if desired, string up several on a coat hanger as a mobile.

Talk about the way you can see this change taking place before your eyes, but in real caterpillars turning into butterflies, the change occurs when it looks as if nothing is happening, as if the caterpillar has just tucked itself up and gone to bed. Wonder together about the way God keeps an eye on us every moment of the day, waking and sleeping, all through our lives, and even carrying on after we die – his loving watchfulness never stops.

Celebration

Rise and shine!

At the blast of the last trumpet… the dead will be raised to live forever. And we will be changed.
1 CORINTHIANS 15:52 (NIRV)

Hear a few stories and comments from the different activities in this session.

This session has been about how things change, secretly and silently, like when we sleep and then wake up refreshed. And sometimes changes can be unexpected and astonishing. Life is full of examples of change like this – it's a sign from God that one day God will change us, ready for heaven.

Tell the story of the life cycle of a butterfly using your hands as indicated in the directions below. Encourage everyone to join you in the story by copying the movements.

A butterfly's life starts as an egg on a leaf. (*Hold an imaginary tiny egg between your finger and thumb.*) It's so small!

The butterfly is huge in comparison, with its fat body, long antennae and beautiful, colourful wings. (*Link your thumbs and flap your fingers to be the wings of a butterfly.*)

What a difference there is between the tiny egg and the big, beautiful butterfly!

Slowly the egg hatches and becomes a caterpillar with its long twisty body, its many, many legs and its bristly, hairy skin. (*Wiggle your index finger up and down in a crawling motion across your other palm, outstretched like a leaf.*)

The butterfly is huge in comparison, with its fat body, long antennae and beautiful, colourful wings. (*Make the butterfly shape again, as above.*)

The caterpillar could never imagine it had anything in common with the butterfly. They are like two completely different animals.

What a difference there is between the wiggly caterpillar and the big, beautiful butterfly!

When the caterpillar has eaten its way through many, many leaves, it finds a cosy place and spins a white 'blanket' around itself so it can go to sleep. It becomes a cocoon, which is white and still and mysterious. (*Curl up the fingers of one hand into a tight fist like a cocoon.*)

The caterpillar was colourful and active and wiggly, compared to this still, white cocoon. The cocoon seems to have nothing in common with the caterpillar. (*Make the caterpillar with your finger and palm again, as above.*)

And the butterfly is still huge in comparison to the cocoon with its fat body, long antennae and beautiful, colourful wings. (*Make the butterfly shape again with your hands, as above.*) They don't seem to have anything in common with each other at all.

What a difference there is between the egg, the caterpillar, the cocoon and the big, beautiful butterfly!

Finally, after many days, the cocoon begins to shake and twist and break up. (*Twist and shake your fist as you say this.*)

And slowly, carefully, miraculously and wonderfully, out of the white cocoon comes a big, beautiful butterfly. (*Make the butterfly again with your two hands.*)

The egg has changed into a caterpillar, which changed into a cocoon and then changed into the butterfly. It's the same creature, but mysteriously changing, again and again!

God has so designed life in this world that there are lots of examples of changes like those in the life cycle of a butterfly, and this is a clue to God's *great surprise*. We can find it in seeds, eggs, frogspawn and even in the tiny baby that grows up to become you and me.

And what is God's great surprise? The surprise is that things change in very unexpected ways.

When we feel stuck, and it seems like bad stuff in our lives will go on forever, we can trust that God can make it all change. This gives us hope – even when someone we love dies.

When we follow Jesus, we start to be changed on the inside and then, even when we grow old and our bodies wear out and die, we are changed on the outside too, with a new body that will never wear out! That new body isn't a ghost or an angel. We know this because after he died, Jesus came back with a new, changed body – leaving his grave clothes behind – to show us what our new body will be like: the new body that belongs to heaven.

Here is a story from the Bible about someone who was near the end of his life but who wasn't sure about what would happen next...

Once there was an old man called Simeon, who lived and worked in the temple in the big city of Jerusalem. He had lived a long life and knew that it would soon be time for him to die. But he was still waiting for something special. He knew that God had one last thing that he wanted him to do. He was sure that he would see God with his own eyes before he died. Yes, amazing as that sounds, that's what God had promised. And so he was waiting and waiting.

One day, Simeon just knew that he should be at the temple at a certain time. He knew that something special was about to happen. He waited and waited, and then he saw a young woman and her husband come with their baby to say thank you to God for a safe birth. And Simeon knew immediately that this baby was the one. It was, of course, baby Jesus. It was God as a baby come to show us how to change, how to love and how to die; and how not to be afraid because we will all be changed in the end.

When Simeon saw Jesus, he held the baby in his hands and sang a song:

Now, I can die in peace
And my long waiting cease.
God's rescuer has come,
A light for everyone.

Simeon felt he could die happily now, that dying would be like having a wonderful rest. He knew that his work on earth was done. Because of this baby, he could trust that one day he would wake refreshed and changed, ready for heaven. He realised that this was true for everybody.

Prayer

Hand out some edible seeds, such as sunflower seeds, and invite everyone to hold a seed in the palm of their hand.

You might like to use the seeds linked to one of the activities in this session.

Encourage everyone to marvel at how tiny the seed is and to think about what a big plant or even a tree it could become. A seed and a plant look like two completely different things and yet they belong together. The seed will change secretly and mysteriously when it has been buried. Similarly, after we have died, we can be changed into a new me and a new you ready for heaven. We will be changed, just like Jesus was when he came back with a new body after his resurrection.

Invite everyone to think about people they know who have died. Give space to be sad but also to be assured that death is not the end and that one day we shall all be changed. It's going to be amazing!

Maybe you can incorporate this call and response as part of this prayer exercise:

Just think how this tiny seed can change into a big plant or huge tree.
It's amazing!

Just think how Jesus lived and died and came back to life again.
It was amazing!

Just think how dying isn't the end but we shall all be changed.
It's going to be amazing!

Song suggestions

'The trumpet shall sound' – Handel (especially the words 'we shall be changed')
'Heaven is a wonderful place' – Kidsource
'One, two, three, Jesus loves me' – Junior Praise and Kidsource
'One more step along the world I go' – Kidsource

Session 4:
Being loved

Messy reflection

Even though I walk through the darkest valley, I will fear no evil... Surely your goodness and love will follow me all the days of my life, and I will dwell in the house of the Lord for ever.

PSALM 23:4, 6 (NIV)

Part of understanding our worth to God is acknowledging how awesomely he has made us, the care he has taken over us, the cost to him of Jesus dying for us and the absurdity of the notion that he would just abandon something that means that much to him before or after death. This session helps us grasp something of how enormously valuable we are to God, and how valuable those members of our family or group of friends are to him, too. It is about reassurance, security and faith that his love has gone on before we were born and will go on in the world to come. We also explore this theme in a different way in the #realme session, available from the Messy Church website.

We also touch on how the 'great cloud of witnesses' is an ever-present reality: we need never be alone in our joy or grief, but are surrounded by those who wish us well. Whether or not we're going through a time of mourning at the moment, it is good to build foundations of these helpful beliefs for when the storms come.

How does this session help people grow in Christ?

We hope that, through the session, families will have an even greater sense of the unconditional love of Christ and of his church. They will feel even more strongly that this is a community in which they belong and are significant. Their sense of self-worth, based not on their looks or abilities but on God's unending care for them, will be reinforced to increase their resilience.

Activities

1 Nail art

You will need: hammers; nails; blocks of relatively soft wood; thread or wool; heart and cross templates; pencils

Mark on the templates where the nails need to go or leave it to people's creativity. Invite people to choose a template that says most about 'love' to them and to draw round that template on a block of wood. They then hammer nails into the shape on the wood and wind thread around the nails in whatever pattern they want to.

Talk about the shape of Jesus' love for us. It has so many shapes to it. But the basic shape is the cross: the cross signifies a kiss; it crosses out all our mistakes and burdens and gives us a fresh start; it shows how much he was prepared to bear for our sake. His love starts before we're born and goes on after we die. He will never stop loving us.

2 No two snowflakes...

You will need: paper circles; scissors; transparent thread; a piece of wire netting or similar, attached to the ceiling but within reach

A joint piece of artwork. Invite people to snip a snowflake from the circles of paper by folding them into halves, then quarters, then eighths, and cutting different shapes from the edges. Unfold them and admire the pattern you've created. Thread the snowflakes on to the clear thread and hang at different heights from the piece of netting so they look as if they are suspended together in mid-air.

Talk about the uniqueness of every snowflake. No two are the same. In the same way, God has made each of us unique. Each one of us matters to him because there has never been anyone like us through the whole of history, and there never will be. He will always treasure us, even after we die.

3 Circle necklace

> **You will need: washers of any size; twine or attractive string; nail varnish or scrapbooking paper (make sure you have patterns that will appeal to all sorts of people); glue or sealant; beads (optional); scissors; craft knife (under supervision)**

Cover the washer, either by painting it thickly on one side with nail varnish and allowing it to dry, or by gluing it to a piece of scrapbooking paper and allowing it to dry for two minutes, then cutting it out as closely to the edge of the washer as you can, including the inside of the washer, with the craft knife. Seal with glue. When dry, thread with a looped knot on to your twine and tie the ends of the twine together to make a necklace. You can thread beads on to the twine just above the washer for further decoration. (Do an images search on 'washer necklace' to see what these look like.)

Talk about the way the circle shape of the washer goes on and on, with no beginning and no end. God's love is like that – it never ends and goes on beyond time, beyond death, beyond anything we can imagine. We are held in this circle of love forever.

4 Hand painting

You will need: face paints; brushes; water

Ask each person who they love. Invite them to write that name on the palm of their hand with face paints. It will smudge and will need washing off before mealtime, but you can keep that name close to you for the rest of the session. Keep looking at it and thinking about how much you love that person and how wonderful they are.

Talk about God's love for us. He says in Isaiah 49:16 (NIV), 'See, I have engraved you on the palms of my hands; your walls are ever before me.' He is talking about Jerusalem. God loved the city so much that he wanted its name on his hand. He loves us just as much. I wonder if he has everyone's names on his hands! He must have very big hands…

5 Shaving foam marbling with hearts

You will need: scissors; paper; newspaper; shaving foam; food colouring or bright paints; a stick; a squeegee; pens

Cut out large heart shapes from the paper. Write or draw on the heart as many people as you can think of who are loved by God. Include people who have died. Include yourself! Squirt shaving foam on to newspaper and spread it out to make a 'bed' on to which you drop colouring/paint. Swirl the colour(s) into the foam's surface. Press the heart down on to the foam, then remove it, turn it foamy side up and scrape off the foam with the squeegee. Allow to dry.

Talk about the way we are surrounded by a great cloud of witnesses to God's love and faithfulness, as the Bible says in Hebrews 12:1. We will never be alone. We are loved by people on this earth and people who have died but are still praising God: they cheer us on too!

6   Psalm flock

You will need: six cut-outs of a shepherd; cartoon sheep cut-outs as follows: 1 A happy sheep, 2 A sleepy sheep, 3 A walking sheep, 4 A sheep with its 'hand' in the shepherd's hand, 5 An eating sheep, 6 Another happy sheep; extra random other sheep; paints; paint brushes; a backdrop with outlines of scenes from Psalm 23 (a pastoral scene – hills, fields, pond; a scary dark road; a banqueting table); print-outs of each verse from Psalm 23 placed in speech bubble shapes

Create a wall display by painting the backdrop in suitable colours, then attaching the six sheep in the appropriate place together with the particular speech bubble and the shepherd that belongs to each one (the numbers above refer to the verses).

Talk about the psalm's description of life with the 'good shepherd', as Jesus described himself. Notice how the shepherd is there in easy, pleasant times and sad, scary times. Jesus will be with us on both sides of death. The rest of the flock of sheep is also with us. How does that make you feel?

7   Junk beauty

You will need: junk; sticky tape; scissors

Make a life-sized person out of junk. It might be easiest to let them 'sit' on a chair or lean against a wall.

Talk about the care, or indeed lack of care, with which this model was made. Do you feel your body was made with care or thrown together out of rubbish? The person who wrote Psalm 139 was blown away by how he was made and said to God, 'I praise you because I am fearfully and wonderfully made' (v. 14, NIV).

8 Round printing

You will need: washable cups; paint in shallow trays or worked into large sponges; large sheets of paper

Invite people to print circles on to the paper in a freestyle pattern, as many as they like.

Talk about the way the circles surround each other and interlink with each other. Are any circles on their own? Link them up with others. God surrounds us with people to love us and look after us all our lives, and he will carry this love and community on after we die. We need never be alone. The roundness of these circles reminds us of the way we are surrounded forever by love.

9 Bubble prayer

You will need: plain water; normal bubble mix; longer-lasting bubble mix; home-made bubble mix; golden syrup or other unbubblable liquid; plenty of bubble blowers; cloths for wiping up

Think about people you love and have as many names as possible at the top of your mind. You could write them down if that helps. Try out the different liquids to see which makes bubbles that last the longest. With each bubble you blow, see how many names of people you love you can say to God out loud before it bursts. Which liquid lets you pray for the most people?

Talk about the way you've just surrounded those people with love and prayer. Other people are surrounding you with love and prayer, too. The bubbles may pop, but God's love for us will never be popped.

10   Cheesy hearts

You will need: recipe for cheese-straw dough and the ingredients (usually butter, plain flour, grated cheese, salt); mixing bowls; spoons; rolling pins; heart-shaped cutters. Gluten-free flour and vegan margarine and cheese are worth considering

Make the dough together or beforehand. Roll it out and cut it into heart shapes. Bake on trays. (There are many sugary edible heart ideas online as alternatives, but sometimes it's good to make something with less processed sugar.)

Talk about the way God loves us now and will never stop loving us, in this life or in the age to come. The cheesy heart will be eaten quickly, but God's love will never end!

Celebration

Forever loved

I have loved you with an everlasting love.
JEREMIAH 31:3 (NIV)

You will need: three big visual aids that represent love – a large heart, a large cross and a large circle; three or four items for valuation (see explanation below)

Which activities did you enjoy? Which one was particularly special for you?

Some of the activities involved circles or crosses or hearts – which shape do you like the best? And why?

I wonder how good you are at guessing the value of something.

Produce three or four items from your home (or borrowed from neighbours) and introduce them. Choose items that have a monetary value you already know, as well as items that are valuable in other ways. They may also be items that have a story attached to them that you can tell, such as a gift from a relative, a family heirloom, something you or your children made, a bargain buy or a souvenir from a holiday. Try to choose items that are contrasting in different ways, and if possible at least one with a surprising monetary value.

After introducing the items, play a game that invites everyone to put these in ascending order of monetary value – in other words, which is worth the least and which is worth the most. Invite people's opinions and comments. Eventually, reveal the true values and also perhaps why; even though something may be worth less in cash, for other reasons it may be very valuable to you.

It seems that everything has a price tag. What something costs or what someone is prepared to pay for it becomes the main way we value everything.

And sometimes this attitude can spill over into how we value people, too. We value people by how much they earn, how much they own, how wealthy they are or how useful or valuable they are to us.

(*Next, invite up three or four people from your Messy congregation – choose people of different ages and gender.*) Now, I wonder, of these people, who owns the most? Who earns the most? Who is the wealthiest? Can we put these people in value order? (*Treat all this in a light-hearted way, though, of course, it is making an important point!*)

When God sees us, God values each one of us equally, and the value God puts on each one of us is way beyond any price tag.

The writer of one of the psalms in the Bible (Psalm 139) tells us that God made each one of us in a beautiful, mysterious and amazing way; that God knows all about us, from even before we were conceived, right through our lives and then beyond death.

(*Introduce the first of your three love shapes – a large heart.*) God knows all about us from the beginning to the end, and even before the beginning and beyond the end. God loves us to bits. Love was the reason God made the world and made us. And each one of us is more valuable than anything to God, and God will do whatever it takes so that we can know and experience that love.

(*Refer back to the people you have invited up.*) There is no amount of money that can match how valuable each of these three people are. But there is one way we can discover how very, very special and valuable each of these lives is to God. Christians believe that love is not just heart-shaped but also cross-shaped.

(*Introduce the second of your three love shapes – a large cross.*) In fact, God did pay a price for each one of us, but it wasn't measured in money or property, or any human terms. Jesus was the price God paid for each one of us. The cross was God's way to make sure we would never ever be cut off from God's love. God's love is cross-shaped.

Now, if we do decide to pay a high price for something (*go back to those items you put up for valuation at the beginning*), isn't it more than likely that you would look after that thing and never let it out of your sight? You would keep it safe forever.

And this is true for each one of us – whatever happens to us. Because God has paid for us with Jesus, then there is nothing, absolutely nothing, that will stop God treasuring us forever… and that includes even after we die.

This is why Christians are so sure that death is not the end. God's love isn't just for this life; it is forever.

(*Introduce the third of your three love shapes – a large circle.*) Love is circle-shaped – love goes on forever. What God made and what God paid for, God will never give up on.

And because God loves us with a heart-shaped, cross-shaped and circle-shaped love, God will keep us through death and will surround us with others who love us too, just as God loves us.

There is a famous poem in the Bible that is often read or sung by Christians to remind themselves that God's love is for all of life and is stronger than death. We call it Psalm 23 and it begins, 'The Lord is my shepherd.' King David probably wrote this song thousands of years ago, and in it he imagines that God is like the very best shepherd ever, caring for us his sheep whatever happens to us. The shepherd was there when we were born into the flock, and he will be there at the end when we move into heaven.

Here are some simple actions to go with each line of the psalm to help us remember it, so it can be a support for us all throughout our lives. It is a psalm that starts in this life with God and ends in heaven with God, and includes all the ups and downs of life in between.

The Lord is my shepherd
Point up and then trace with one finger the curve of a crook, which you then 'hold'.

He gives me everything I need
Hold out both arms as if receiving gifts.

He lets me lie down in fields of green grass
Rest the side of your head on your hands.

He leads me beside quiet waters
Walk on the spot and listen with one hand cupped to one ear.

He gives me new strength
Lift up hands and arms slowly.

He guides me in the right paths for the honour of his name
Trace a path ahead with one hand and arm.

Even though I walk through the darkest valley
*Walk on the spot, pulling an imaginary cape around you and
   looking around.*

I will not be afraid
Hold up one hand as a stop sign.

You are with me
Reach out with one hand as if to hold on to someone.

Your shepherd's rod and staff comfort me
Hold these imaginary weapons/tools, one in each hand.

You prepare a feast for me right in front of my enemies
Sit down at an imaginary table.

You pour oil on my head
Touch your head gently with one hand.

My cup runs over
Lift up an imaginary cup to your lips.

I'm sure that your goodness and mercy will follow me all the
   days of my life
Touch your heart and then make the sign of the cross over yourself.

And I will live in the house of the Lord forever
Describe a big circle in front of you, with the fingers of one hand.

Prayer

You could make this version of Psalm 23 your final prayer for this celebration, or else you might like to go back to the three love shapes and use them with this next prayer, inviting everyone to make the shape each time with the fingers of both hands:

(Make a heart shape with the index fingers and thumbs from both hands.) Thank you, Father God, that you made us and will love us forever and for always.

(Make a cross shape with your two index fingers.) Thank you, Father God, that you paid Jesus for us and will love us forever and always.

(Make a circle shape, linking up the fingertips of both hands and rounding this into a circle) Thank you, Father God, that you surround us with people who love us and with a love that is stronger than death, and all because you will love us forever and for always. Amen

Song suggestions

'God's love is like a circle' (to the tune of 'Puff the Magic Dragon')
'O the deep, deep love of Jesus' – Mission Praise
'There is a redeemer' – Mission Praise
'Abba Father' – Junior Praise
'I'm special' – Graham Kendrick (Junior Praise)

Session 5:
Finding safe spaces

Messy reflection

One thing I ask from the Lord, this only do I seek: that I may dwell in the house of the Lord all the days of my life, to gaze on the beauty of the Lord and to seek him in his temple. For in the day of trouble he will keep me safe in his dwelling; he will hide me in the shelter of his sacred tent and set me high upon a rock.

PSALM 27:4–5 (NIV)

We all feel the need to hide away at times. This is a basic human response to feeling vulnerable and afraid, and hiding is our natural response to thinking about death. It's also a feature of bereavement. When someone we love dies, those of us who are left behind can feel a whole range of emotions. As part of the healing ministry of a church, we can make a safe place to express these feelings and simply be alongside people in their grief as an expression of Christ himself being alongside them.

When people need to hide away, we can support them until they feel ready to venture forth. We can make safe spaces in our buildings, our conversations and our attitudes for them to find the 'hiding place' where they can have the headspace to process upsetting stuff at their own pace.

In Messy Church, we can experiment with the different expressions of emotions, not just through words but through the different senses, so that young and old have an opportunity to mark what they are going through. As well as the activities suggested below, simple opportunities to light a candle in memory of someone or to hang a prayer on a prayer tree are valuable services that we can provide.

How does this session help people grow in Christ?

The session will help people understand and trust that Jesus makes dark places light and scary places safe, and that he is always there – accessible, compassionate and reliable, a rock in times of trouble.

Activities

1 Den building

You will need: anything you have to hand with which to build dens – large cardboard boxes, old sheets, clothes horses, etc.; wood and tools (if you can supervise safely)

Make dens from the materials available.

Talk about safe places where we can go and hide – they might be physical places like this den or places in our heads where we feel safe and feel God is close. When someone we love dies, we need a safe place like this to hide in when we're feeling sad.

2 Safe spot

You will need: clear glass nuggets (check one side is flattish); glue that dries clear; maps of your local area; world maps; scissors; magnetic strips

Invite people to think of a place in the world where they feel particularly close to God, safe, peaceful and at home. It might be local or further afield. If there is nowhere geographical, ask them to think of an imagined place in their head. Find the place on the appropriate map; draw around a nugget, with the correct place at the centre of the nugget shape and cut it out carefully. Glue it to the base of the nugget and, when the glue is dry, attach a small piece of magnetic strip to the back so it can be stuck to an appropriate surface. (If it is an imagined place, draw around the nugget and draw the imagined place on to a piece of plain paper.)

Talk about why these places feel safe. Talk about our need to hide in a safe place like these when someone we love dies. We might be able to go there physically for 'time out' with God, or we might give ourselves time out there in our imagination. This can restore our courage and help us face the future.

3 Bother box

You will need: matchboxes; coloured pens; paper heart shapes small enough to fit inside the matchbox; a list of short Bible verses as below (all are from the NIV; you could print these out if your congregation hates writing)

Fear and worry:
Do not be afraid; do not be discouraged, for the Lord your God will be with you wherever you go.
JOSHUA 1:9

The Lord is my light and my salvation – whom shall I fear? The Lord is the stronghold of my life – of whom shall I be afraid?
PSALM 27:1

When I am afraid, I put my trust in you.
PSALM 56:3

When you lie down, you will not be afraid; when you lie down, your sleep will be sweet.
PROVERBS 3:24

Surely God is my salvation; I will trust and not be afraid. The Lord, the Lord himself, is my strength and my defence; he has become my salvation.

ISAIAH 12:2

Do not be afraid, land of Judah; be glad and rejoice. Surely the Lord has done great things!

JOEL 2:21

Everyone will sit under their own vine and under their own fig-tree, and no one will make them afraid, for the Lord Almighty has spoken.

MICAH 4:4

So don't be afraid; you are worth more than many sparrows.

MATTHEW 10:31

But Jesus immediately said to them: 'Take courage! It is I. Don't be afraid.'

MATTHEW 14:27

The women hurried away from the tomb, afraid yet filled with joy, and ran to tell his disciples.

MATTHEW 28:8

Jesus told him, 'Don't be afraid; just believe.'

MARK 5:36

But the angel said to her, 'Do not be afraid, Mary, you have found favour with God.'

LUKE 1:30

Then Jesus said to Simon, 'Don't be afraid; from now on you will fish for people.'

LUKE 5:10

Do not be afraid, little flock, for your Father has been pleased
to give you the kingdom.
LUKE 12:32

There is no fear in love. But perfect love drives out fear.
1 JOHN 4:18

Grief:
Come to me, all you who are weary and burdened, and I will
give you rest.
MATTHEW 11:28

Jesus wept.
JOHN 11:35

Even though I walk through the darkest valley, I will fear no evil,
for you are with me... [you] comfort me.
PSALM 23:4

May your unfailing love be my comfort.
PSALM 119:76

Comfort, comfort my people, says your God.
ISAIAH 40:1

I will turn their mourning into gladness; I will give them comfort
and joy instead of sorrow.
JEREMIAH 31:13

Blessed are those who mourn, for they will be comforted.
MATTHEW 5:4

Do not let your hearts be troubled. You believe in God; believe
also in me.
JOHN 14:1

Praise be to… the Father of compassion and the God of all comfort, who comforts us in all our troubles.
2 CORINTHIANS 1:3–4

You will grieve, but your grief will turn to joy.
JOHN 16:20

'He will wipe every tear from their eyes. There will be no more death' or mourning or crying or pain.
REVELATION 21:4

Say to people that there are all sorts of things in life that bother us (you don't need to emphasise death and dying, but just receive it if someone brings it up). But there is always help to get us through this difficult time. We are never alone. God's love is there surrounding us, and the Bible reminds us of this. On the outside of the box, label the words 'Bother Box' and write short phrases or draw things that bother you at the moment. Decorate any space left on the outside of your box. On each paper heart, copy a verse from the list that will comfort you or give you hope when you are bothered or down. Keep it for when you feel upset and need some comfort.

Talk about how one of the things a church does is to be there for you through good times and bad. You can always be honest with people there. You don't have to pretend. (You may have to practise this as a church, however!)

4 Safe space

You will need: water bomb balloons; liquid paint; large sheet of paper; masking tape

An uber-messy one! Prepare the paper by marking out a shape with masking tape: a heart or a cross is good, but anything that symbolises a safe space. Fill water bombs with paint and take it in turns to throw bombs at the large sheet of paper. After the barrage, peel off the masking tape and reveal the 'sacred' or untouched space on the paper.

Talk about the way it can feel when a lot is being thrown at you. What do you do or need to do to keep a space that isn't marked by those things? Do you need to make space for a walk in a beautiful place, for example, or make time to read a little bit of the Bible or to pray?

5 Umbrella challenge

You will need: protective clothing in several sizes; old umbrellas; liquid paint

Challenge people to stand underneath the umbrella while paint (or water if you need it to be a little cheaper) is poured over the umbrella. Who can keep cleanest or driest?

Talk about the way people need a shelter when bad things happen to them, like a family member dying. They need to be overshadowed with love to help them deal with the pain. Who in your family, church or group of friends is most like an umbrella?

6 Shoe art

You will need: a selection of old shoes; beads; glue; needles and thread; acrylic paints and brushes; ribbons; stickers. If you have time to emulsion the shoes with white paint and allow to dry beforehand, that makes an easier base to work from.

Decorate the old shoes to turn them into works of art.

Talk about the phrase 'walking in someone else's shoes' and what it means. Have you ever known somebody who has made the effort to see things from your point of view, to walk in your shoes? Have you ever done that for someone else, particularly someone who is hurting? What difference can it make?

7 Pillowcase

You will need: plain pillowcases; fabric paints or pens; irons; ironing boards

Copy part of Revelation 21:4 – 'God will wipe away every tear from their eyes' – on to the pillowcase in fabric pen. Then decorate the whole pillowcase. Fix the decoration by ironing it or do whatever the instructions suggest.

Talk about how bedtime can be a sad time when you've had a miserable day. It's good to tell God about it and to hold on to his promise that in the new heaven and the new earth, everything will be perfect, as your pillowcase reminds you.

8 Felting feelings

You will need: felting wool; water; liquid soap; towels

Make the wool into felt by soaking it in water and rubbing in soap, then distressing it over and over again between your hands. It takes ten minutes or more, so plenty of time to chat. The soap breaks down the fibres in the wool and they 'felt' together. Form it into a small ball, the size of a marble and rinse out the soap in lots of water. Allow it to dry, then use it to decorate a bag or as a bead on a necklace. There are lots of online instructions and videos if you've never done it.

Talk about times we've felt as if we're being broken down and how hard that can feel. Paul often felt like that but could still say, 'For I am convinced that neither death nor life, neither angels nor demons, neither the present nor the future, nor any powers, neither height nor depth, nor anything else in all creation, will be able to separate us from the love of God that is in Christ Jesus our Lord' (Romans 8:38–39, NIV).

9   A meaning meal

You will need: samples of foods that are (separately) bitter, sweet, salty, hot, tough, smooth and so on – in other words, flavours or textures that have associated emotions (salty for salt tears, smooth for an easy happy sensation and so forth), if necessary cut into small cubes; teaspoons; plates; cups

Remind everyone about the Passover or Seder meal that Jesus ate on the Thursday night before he died, where every food had a meaning about God's rescue plan in the past. Invite people to make up a 'meaning meal' to tell the story of an experience they've been through recently, using the food and drink available to describe it.

Talk about the experience they create and describe, but also invite them to think about people who are going through a very different experience from their own. Talk about how good it is to keep talking about happy AND sad times together.

10   Beast box

You will need: twigs and sticks; old plastic water bottles; string

Make a minibeast home by cutting the base off a bottle and wedging as many twigs as you can into the top section until they are fixed into place. Tie string around the bottle so it can be tied to a suitable wall or fence outside your home. If left undisturbed, small creatures will soon find their way into it to shelter. (If you have someone with the right skills and tools, you might make bird boxes instead.)

Talk about the insects finding a safe place to hide from things that would hurt them. Talk about the way Christians know God as a hiding place and run to him in terrible times. The Bible says, 'You are my hiding-place; you will protect me from trouble and surround me with songs of deliverance' (Psalm 37, NIV). Have you ever tried this?

Celebration

A safe place

> You are my hiding-place.
>
> PSALM 32:7 (NIV)

Begin by talking about the activities and which ones people enjoyed. Was there one activity that meant something special to them? Bring out the link to special places of safety or shelter as the main theme.

Listen, listen... the rain is coming!

Invite everyone to begin drumming with one finger on the palm of the opposite hand, then with two fingers, three and four. The combined drumming will sound like a growing rainstorm.

Yes, it's a rainstorm! Imagine you are out in the open, you haven't brought your waterproofs with you, you haven't got an umbrella and so... you run... putting up your collars if you have them... running for the nearest shelter!

We need a safe, dry place when the storm comes.

Listen, listen... the shouting is getting louder!

Invite everyone to begin by whispering nonsense words and then getting louder and louder until everyone is shouting. It will sound like a frightening wall of angry noise.

Yes, sometimes there are so many voices telling us to go this way or that, urging us to do this or that, that it becomes unbearable; you can't stand it anymore. You put your hands over your ears to block out the noise. You want a place to hide, a safe place from all that sound.

We need a safe, quiet place when the world's noise gets too much.

Listen, listen… there is crying.

Invite people to begin by sobbing quietly, wiping imaginary tears from their eyes, but then sobbing louder and louder until the sadness is overwhelming.

Yes, sometimes you are so worried or sad that you start to cry. You just want a quiet corner in which to hug yourself. You want a place to escape – a hiding place where you can breathe again and find comfort beyond your tears.

We need a safe, comforting place when worries or sadness threaten to overwhelm us.

I think all of us will recognise these situations and feelings. Maybe some of you are actually in that situation right now, looking for a safe place to be, a shelter from the storm, a hiding place from the noise and a comforting place in a time of deep sadness.

And God knows how you feel.

One of the Bible writers puts it like this: 'The Lord is a mighty tower where his people can run for safety' (Proverbs 18:10, CEV).

Sometimes our feelings of worry or sadness can be overwhelming. We might feel empty, lost and alone. That is a normal part of life – even Jesus felt that way sometimes, and that means he knows how we feel. The Bible tells us that he cried his heart out when one of his best friends called Lazarus died. And God knows we need a safe place to be in such times – a place of shelter and a safe home.

And God offers us just this – a hiding place when we need it… and it will be different and special for every one of us.

Invite everyone to discover the specialness of this place using their hands, following the directions below:

Stick out the index finger prominently above one hand.
This is us – you and me – each unique as the fingerprint on the end of this finger.

Bend the finger low.
And this is us when hard times come: sad because of losing someone or something precious; worried about the unknown; and afraid of danger.

Overshadow the bent finger now with the palm of your other hand.
God promises to shelter us. The Bible says, 'You are my fortress, my place of safety... He will spread his wings over you' (Psalm 91:2, 4, CEV).

Now wrap the fingers of your other hand around the bent index finger but not touching that finger.
God promises to keep us safe. Jesus said: 'I have a place prepared for you. I have gone before you to make a home ready for you' (see John 14).

Now invite those near to each other to provide sheltering hands around the bent index finger, doing this in turn for each other.
God promises a home for us alongside others who will help God keep us safe. In the Bible we read: 'The Lord has promised that he will not leave us or desert us' (Hebrews 13:5, CEV) and 'Comfort one another' (1 Thessalonians 4:18, RSV).

Not only does God offer us a safe place but God uses others, who care about us, to create safe places for each of us in times of distress.

It happened for the boy in this story:

Once there was a young teenager who was restless and rebellious. He wanted to break free and live his life far away from the restrictions of his family home. So he took his share of the family fortune and left home as soon as he could.

Away from those who loved him, the teenager did as he pleased, spending the money extravagantly and welcoming all the pleasures that life could offer, the good and the bad. He lived on the wild edge of life, until one day his money ran out. He became penniless and friendless. He had lost everything – all his money, his friends, his home and then even his dignity: he ended up on the scrapheap, in a dead-end job that everyone despised.

Then, in the eye of this storm of sadness and disaster, he remembered. He remembered the safe place he had had at home but which he had left behind. He remembered the sheltering love that his parents and family friends had given him. And he longed to be in that safe place again. He came to his senses. He set out for home, shaken and shattered by all that he had experienced and not even sure he deserved to be safe again.

But the father was looking out for him; the father had never given up on him; the father had always kept a safe place ready for him to return to. And the father ran to meet him, wrapped his arms around him and welcomed him back into the shelter of the family home. And the community gathered around him, throwing a party, to welcome him back into a safe place again.

That was part of a story that Jesus once told. A story that helps us remember that God is always ready to welcome us back into his safekeeping, whatever has happened to us.

The writers of the Psalms put it like this: 'Our Lord… you have been our home' (Psalm 90:1, CEV) and 'You are my place of safety' (Psalm 119:114, CEV).

Christians believe that those who have died are safe with God for ever, but they also believe that we too can experience a taste of that safety here on earth – a place we can go with our sadness and pain.

And in that place of safety, we can slowly learn to become brave and live fully again.

Prayer

Return to the image of the index finger bent above one hand and allow it to uncurl slowly upright again.

Give space for some quiet prayer and reflection in response to the following:

I wonder where your safe place is, when the storms of sadness and loss come.

I wonder how we can make safe places for others when they are facing the storms of sadness and loss.

I wonder what God is saying to you today about the safety God offers us.

Song suggestions

'Rock of Ages' – Augustus Toplady (maybe a selected verse or two)
'The name of the Lord is a strong tower' – traditional
'Blessed be the name of the Lord' – Matt Redman
'Be still and know that I am God'– traditional

Further resources

Books

Jenny Album, *Tell Me about Heaven, Grandpa Rabbit!*
(Little Boo, 2014).

Alan Durant, *Always and Forever* (Picture Corgi, 2013).

Glenda Fredman, *Death Talk: Conversations with children and families* (Karnac, 1997).

Laura Olivieri, *Where Are You?* (Lulu.com, 2007).

Michael Rosen and Quentin Blake, *Michael Rosen's Sad Book*
(Walker Books, 2011).

Doris Stickney, *Water Bugs and Dragonflies* (Pilgrim Press, 2009).

Web resources

- Dying Matters: **dyingmatters.org/sites/default/files/user/images/Resources/Promo%20materials/Leaflet_8_Web.pdf**
- Marie Curie: **mariecurie.org.uk/blog/10-questions-children-ask-about-death-dying/142040**
- SeeSaw: **seesaw.org.uk/Resources**
- Centre for Theology and Ministry, Australia: **ctmresourcing.org.au/building-emotional-health-and-wellbeing**
- A moving story: **theguardian.com/lifeandstyle/2017/dec/30/mother-sons-prepared-death-losing-cope**

Notes

1   Abbot Parry (trans.), *The Rule of Saint Benedict* (Gracewing, 1990).
2   Sarah Young, 'Messy desks could be a sign of genius, say researchers', *Independent*, 11 July 2017, **independent.co.uk/life-style/messy-desks-genius-sign-work-environment-creative-interesting-university-minnesota-a7834786.html**
3   This is the literal translation of John 1:14.
4   **ncpc.org.uk**
5   **dyingmatters.org**
6   'You, me and the big C' blog: **bbc.co.uk/programmes/p0608649**.
7   **dyingmatters.org**
8   **stchristophers.org.uk/schools-project**
9   Victoria Slater and Joanna Collicutt, 'Living well in the end times (LWET): a project to research and support churches' engagement with issues of death and dying', *Practical Theology*, 11 (2018): 1176–188.
10 Sally Goddard Blythe, *The Genius of Natural Childhood* (Hawthorne Press, 2011), Kindle version.
11 **churchofenglandfunerals.org/gravetalk**
12 Diocese of Oxford (2019), 'Death and life: Christian resources for living well in the light of mortality': **deathlife.org.uk**.
13 Joanna Collicutt and Martyn Payne, 'The ageless kingdom of God', *Church Times*, 11 December 2015.
14 Psalm 148:12
15 *The Fellowship of the Ring* (2001), dir. Peter Jackson.
16 'Safeguarding the convoy: a call to action from the Campaign to End Loneliness' (Campaign to End Loneliness and Age UK Oxfordshire, 2011): **campaigntoendloneliness.org/wp-content/uploads/Safeguarding-the-Convoy.-A-call-to-action-from-the-Campaign-to-End-Loneliness-1.pdf**.
17 Matthew 19:14
18 Shel Silverstein, 'The Little Boy and the Old Man', quoted in Holly Catterton Allen and Christine Lawton Ross, *Intergenerational Christian Formation* (IVP, 2012), p. 133.

19 Jerome Berryman, *Godly Play: An imaginative approach to religious education* (Augsburg, 1991), p. 57.

20 Children who have mental health conditions, a history of disrupted attachment or abuse or special educational needs are likely to respond in less predictable ways. When carrying out activities with these children, it is important to be guided by their parents or guardians, who should have a good idea of their ability to tolerate mild degrees of challenge or stress.

21 Martyn Payne, 'Halloween – trick or treat?', **eden.co.uk/blog/ halloween-trick-or-treat-p123009.**

22 Kate Lyons, 'Boys trapped in Thai cave write letters telling families "don't worry"', *The Guardian*, 7 July 2018, **theguardian.com/ news/2018/jul/07/boys-trapped-in-thai-cave-write-letters-telling- families-dont-worry**

23 With thanks to Elizabeth Thomson.

24 Song of Songs 8:6

25 'Gone from my sight' (multiple attributions).

26 Jill Murphy, *Peace at Last* (MacMillan, 2007).

27 *Common Worship Pastoral Services* (Church House, 2011), p. 323.

28 Quoted by Michael Barbato in Elizabeth Mackinlay, *Aging, Spirituality and Palliative Care* (Haworth Press, 2006), p. 112.

29 Extract translated by John Lampard in *Go Forth, Christian Soul: The biography of a prayer* (Wipf and Stock, 2005), p. 2.

30 Mary Oliver, *New and Selected Poems* (Beacon Press, 1993), p. 10.

31 For some helpful resources, see SeeSaw: **seesaw.org.uk.**

32 Colin Brazier, 'Let funerals be sad', *The Spectator*, 21 July 2018.

In *Messy Hospitality*, Lucy Moore demonstrates how hospitality can be practised in Messy Church and other church contexts to promote mission and faith formation, addressing the theology of hospitality and how it can be expressed at the welcome table, the activity table, the Lord's Table and the meal table, and in the home. Also included are insights from the secular hospitality industry, how to train Messy Church teams in hospitality, audit-style questions for the reader to apply in their own context and five complete session outlines for Messy Churches.

Messy Hospitality
Changing communities through fun, food, friendship and faith
Lucy Moore
978 0 85746 415 6 £9.99

brfonline.org.uk

In *Messy Togetherness*, Martyn Payne looks at Messy Church as an all-age expression of church and the benefits of this to the church community. He explores current thinking about faith development, gives a biblical rationale for the all-age approach, offers practical advice and shares stories and ideas from across the Messy Church network. The book also contains three complete outlines for Messy Church sessions (from the Old Testament, the gospels and the epistles), which offer Bible stories with insights into what it means to be intergenerational as church.

Messy Togetherness
Being intergenerational in Messy Church
Martyn Payne
978 0 85746 461 3 £8.99

brfonline.org.uk

Get Messy! is a four-monthly subscription resource for Messy Church leaders. Each issue contains four session outlines (one per month), including planning sheets and take-home handouts, together with information on the latest resources and events. It also seeks to encourage and refresh Messy Church leaders by providing monthly Bible studies, stories from other Messy Churches, a youth column and a problem page.

Get Messy!

Session material, news, stories and inspiration for the Messy Church community

£4.60 per issue

brfonline.org.uk

Doing church differently

BRF's Messy Church is a form of church that involves creativity, celebration and hospitality, and enables people of all ages to belong to Christ together through their local church. It is particularly aimed at people who have never belonged to a church before.

Find out more at **messychurch.org.uk**

 brf.org.uk